PHONICS THEY USE
Words for Reading and Writing

Second Edition

Patricia M. Cunningham
Wake Forest University

 HarperCollins*CollegePublishers*

Acquisitions Editor/Executive Editor: Christopher Jennison
Project Coordination, Text and Cover Design: York Production Services
Art Coordination: York Production Services
Electronic Production Manager: Christine Pearson
Electronic Page Makeup: York Production Services
Printer and Binder: R. R. Donnelley and Sons Company
Cover Printer: The Lehigh Press, Inc.

Phonics They Use: Words for Reading and Writing

Copyright © 1995 by HarperCollins College Publishers

Library of Congress Cataloging-in-Publication Data

Cunningham, Patricia Marr.
    Phonics They Use: Words for Reading and Writing / Patricia M.
Cunningham. — 2nd ed.
        p.   cm.
    Includes index.
    ISBN 0-673-99087-7
    1. Reading   (Elementary) — Phonetic method.   I. Title
LB1573.3.C86   1995
372.4' 145 — dc20
                                                            94-34943
                                                            CIP

12 13 14 15 16 -DOC- 01 00 99 98 97

CONTENTS

Time Flies When You're Having Fun, or It's Time for a Second Edition Already?

My eighty-two-year-old mother says that when time starts going faster, it is a sure sign you are getting older! I'd rather not believe her on this but since she is getting smarter every year, I do have to wonder!

Actually, I am both astonished and grateful to have the chance to do this second edition of *Phonics They Use*. When the book first appeared in 1991, very few reading gurus—my best friends included—gave it much of a chance. Phonics was not something you talked about, and most people believed (or pretended to believe) that teachers had stopped doing it! As far as I know, *Phonics They Use* didn't get a single review, negative or positive, in any professional journal.

The teacher underground is a powerful force, however. Little by little, word spread. Teachers bought it and loaned it to their most trusted friends. Some teachers felt the need to hide the book—or at least the cover. One teacher I met at a conference praised the book but suggested that I should not have used "the P word—Phonics"—in the title. "People just don't understand" she said. "When they think of phonics, they think of grunting and groaning and endless worksheets. I explained to my principal that this phonics was not like that. She said she understood but asked me to keep the book out of sight because visitors might get the wrong idea!"

Despite the fact that as the 1990s began phonics was not politically correct, teachers bought the book and appreciated the concrete suggestions for teaching phonics in ways consistent with holistic reading and writing. My mail attested to the dedication and creativity of elementary teachers. This Christmas, I got holiday cards containing pictures of word walls, children in sandwich-style letter cards "becoming the letters" as they made words, class-authored books of tongue twisters, and numerous other spinoffs from some of the suggested activities in *Phonics They Use*. These treasures sent to me by busy teachers who made time to gather them up and send them to me were the Christmas gifts I appreciated most. So it was with a glad and happy heart that I sat down at my MacPowerbook the day after Christmas to begin this revision.

This second edition has been greatly influenced by the comments and suggestions made by teachers who used the first edition. There are a number of new activities and some new twists on some of the older ones. One thing I have learned since writing the first edition is that teachers try to integrate their word activities with their literature and other themes. Thus I have included more examples of activities connected to favorite books and science and social studies topics.

I am even more convinced than I was while writing the first edition that spelling and decoding are "two faces of a coin" and that activities which help children develop their word knowledge move them through the stages toward conventional spelling. I have added sections on word sorting, using visual information and dictionaries to determine the correct spelling, and linking spelling with meaning.

Fluency is an issue I have become more concerned about in the past few years. Fluency is the ability to read quickly with comprehension and expression. Fluency develops as children do lots of easy reading, something many children do not do much of if their schools have adopted the newer— more literature-based but harder—basal readers. I have included some suggestions for developing fluency along with suggestions for easy books available in most school libraries.

In most classrooms I visit, teachers now appreciate the difference between assessment and testing. Anecdotal records and portfolios are actually being used as authentic assessment devices. I have included in this second edition some ways to assess children's developing word knowledge which are consistent with our more realistic approach to determining who knows what and documenting progress.

Finally, I have learned that, contrary to popular opinion, teachers have theories about how children learn, and they do care about research! Whenever I make a presentation to teachers, I always include the most relevant research. I then show how the practical activities are consistent with this research and try to give the teachers a sense of how to judge other activities they might be using. Invariably, teachers come up to me after the presentation and want to know where they can find out more about the theory and research base for effective phonics and spelling instruction. I have decided that when people say teachers don't want research, they really mean teachers don't want research from which they have to infer all the practical applications. Research instead of practical suggestions is not appreciated by most practicing teachers! But when linked to practical activities, teachers appreciate and can make sense of the theory and research. For this reason, I have included an adaptation of a research summary I made at a National Reading Conference meeting at the end of this edition.

Writing this second edition, I am even more indebted to teachers than I was while writing the first. Most of the changes and additions have come from their comments and suggestions. Assuming my mother is right and that time is going to go even faster in the next several years, I can only ask my readers to keep those cards and letters—pictures and samples—coming because before we know it, I will need some fresh ideas! I apologize to those of you who suggested I take *Phonics* out of the title. *Phonics* is a good word—we can do good phonics instruction. Perhaps, through our combined efforts, no one will have to hide the fourth or fifth edition!

INTRODUCTION

"They know the skills. They just don't use them!" These words express the frustration felt by many teachers who spend endless hours teaching children phonics only to find that the skills that are demonstrated on a worksheet or a mastery test often don't get used where they matter—in reading and writing. Because poor readers have so much difficulty applying the phonics skills they learn, many experts have called for an end to phonics instruction: "Just let them read and write and they will figure out whatever they need to know." Now, everyone agrees that children must read and write; in fact, if you had to choose between teaching either phonics or reading and writing, you would always choose reading and writing. But you don't have to make a choice. You can engage the children's minds and hearts in reading good literature and finding their own voices as authors *and,* at the same time, teach them how our alphabetic language works!

All good readers have the ability to look at a word they have never seen before and assign it a probable pronunciation. Witness your ability to pronounce these made-up words:

bame   **spow**   **perzam**   **chadulition**

Now, of course, you weren't truly reading, because having pronounced these words, you didn't access any meaning. But if you were in the position of most young readers who have many more words in their listening-meaning vocabularies than in their sight-reading vocabularies, you would often meet words familiar in speech but unfamiliar in print. The ability you demonstrated to rapidly figure out the pronunciation of unfamiliar-in-print words would enable you to make use of your huge store of familiar-in-speech words and thus access meaning.

Before we go on, how did you pronounce the made-up word, *spow?* Did it rhyme with *cow* or with *snow?* Because the English language does not assign one sound to each letter, there are different ways to pronounce certain letter patterns, but the number of different ways is limited; moreover, with real words, unlike made-up words, your speaking vocabulary lets you know which pronunciation to assign.

Not only do beginning readers use their phonics knowledge to enable them to read words they have not seen before, this same knowledge enables them to write. Had I dictated the four made-up words to you and asked you to write them, you would have spelled them in a way which is reasonably close to the way I spelled them. You might have spelled the first one *baim* and the last one *chedulition,* but your "invented" spelling would have resembled my made-up spelling to a remarkable degree.

All good readers and writers develop this ability to come up with pronunciations and spellings for words they have never read or written before. Many poor readers do not. Good readers and writers do, indeed, read and write, and, as they read and write, they figure out how our system works. Poor readers and writers need to read and write, but they also need to have their attention directed to words and the way these words work, so that they can make rapid progress in reading and writing. This book is about how to direct children's attention toward letters and sounds to enable them to *use strategies* not learn skills.

The distinction between strategy and skill is blurred, at best. But I would like to share with you how I distinguish them. To me, a strategy is something you do to accomplish some goal. People develop strategies to get things done and often they don't have words to describe what they are doing. Strategies almost never have rules or jargon attached to them. Strategies are not usually something you know. Rather, they are something you *do!* Some examples might help to clarify this important distinction.

When good readers see a word they never before have seen in print, they stop momentarily and study the word by looking at every letter in a left-to-right sequence. As they look at all the letters, they are not thinking a sound for each letter because good readers know that sounds are determined not by individual letters but by letter patterns. Good readers look for patterns of letters they have seen together before and then search their mental word stores looking for words with similar letter patterns. If the new word is a long word, they "chunk" it. That is, they put letters together that make familiar chunks.

Based on their careful inspection of the letters and their search through their mental store for words with the same letter patterns, good readers *try out* a pronunciation. They then go back and reread the sentence that contained the unfamiliar-in-print word and see if their pronunciation makes sense given the meaning they are getting from the context of surrounding words. If the pronunciation they came up with makes sense, they continue reading. If not, they look again at all the letters of the unfamiliar word and see what else would "look like this and make sense."

Imagine a young boy reading this sentence: *The man was poisoned by lead.* Now imagine that he pauses at the last word and then pronounces *lead* so that it rhymes with *bead.* His eyes then glance back and he quickly rereads the sentence and realizes that "it doesn't sound right." He studies all the letters of *lead* again and searches for similar letter patterns in his mental word store. Perhaps he now accesses words such as *head* and *bread.* This gives him another possible pronunciation for this letter pattern. He tries this pronunciation, quickly rereads, realizes his sentence now "sounds right" and continues reading.

From this scenario, we can infer the strategies this good reader used to successfully decode an unfamiliar-in-print word:

1. Recognize that this is an unfamiliar word and look at all the letters in a left-to-right sequence.

2. Search your mental store for similar letter patterns and the sounds associated with them and come up with a probable pronunciation.

3. Reread the sentence to cross-check your probable pronunciation with meaning. If meaning confirms pronunciation, continue reading. If not, try again! Had this unfamiliar-in-print word been a big word, the reader would have had to use a fourth strategy:

4. Chunk the word by putting letters together which usually go together in the words you know.

These four strategies—looking at all the letters in a left-to-right sequence, matching letter patterns with pronunciation, chunking big words, and cross-checking are supported by numerous research studies and by commonsense observations of what we, as good readers, do. (This is not a book about research but this is a book based on research. The relevant research can be found at the end of this book.)

Now, with these strategies clearly in mind, let's briefly consider the purported phonics skills we teach children:

> Sound out all the letters in the word, then, blend them together to see what you have.
>
> When an *a* is followed by a consonant and an *e,* try the long sound of *a.*
>
> When there are two consonants that are not a digraph in the middle of a word, divide between them.
>
> The second syllable of a three- or four-syllable word is often unaccented.

I could list many more, but these few examples should suffice. Poor readers don't use such skills because they do not represent the strategies good readers use. Rather, the listed skills are an attempt to describe our system and explain it. The strategies are what you do when you come to a word you don't recognize or can't spell. Strategies are mental processes you use to do something you want to do. And yes, it appears that good readers learn these strategies—on their own—from their reading and writing, without (and sometimes, in spite of) our instruction, but, some children don't. They never figure out how you do it! They sound every letter and then can't blend what they have. They try to remember what the *e* does to the *a* and whether those two consonants in the middle are a digraph but then they don't know what to do with that knowledge! This book is written for those children and for teachers who want to teach those children.

The book describes activities which I and numerous teachers have used to help children who have not figured out the strategies on their own and who don't know "what you do!" In writing this book and in developing and collecting the activities to include, I have tried to follow these five principles:

1. Because children are "active" learners, they should not just sit and listen or watch but should be actively engaged in doing something!

2. Because children are at all different stages in their word knowledge, a good activity has "something for everyone." It begins with a warm-up (a very easy activity) and ends with a challenge (to stretch our stars!). I call these multilevel activities.

3. Because children have different styles, modalities, and ways in which they learn most easily, activities will include as much variety as possible—chanting, singing, rhythm, rhyme, drama, movement, games, and so on.

4. Jargon and rules should be kept to the absolute minimum required to communicate.

5. The sole purpose for reading and writing words is to enable reading and writing. Daily reading and writing must be how children spend the vast majority of their time.

There are four chapters in this book. Chapter One details the incredibly large amount of information children who come from homes in which literacy is a priority bring to school with them. More importantly, this first chapter describes activities that real teachers working with real children have used in trying to make sure all children have the foundation needed to learn to read and write. Although Chapter One will be particularly useful to preschool and kindergarten teachers, first- and second-grade teachers who have children who are not making progress in reading and writing often need to include some of these foundational activities in their classrooms.

Chapter Two describes activities for helping children learn to decode and spell regular one-syllable words. Activities include many suggestions for helping children associate sounds with consonant, digraph, and blend letters as well as activities for helping children get control of our complex vowel system.

Because English contains numerous irregular words—those not pronounced or spelled in the way you would expect them to be—and because these irregular words are also the most common words, Chapter Three describes specific activities you can use with children to speed them along the route to immediate and automatic recognition and spelling of such highly frequent words. Chapters Two and Three will be most useful to first- and second-grade teachers; those who teach older children who lack strategies in one-syllable decoding or in reading and spelling highly frequent words will find these strategies also work for older children.

Chapter Four is devoted to the special problems some students experience as they encounter polysyllabic, or, *big,* words in their reading and writing. A variety of activities for helping children become independent with big words are also described in Chapter Four. The activities described are probably most on target for average third and fourth graders but have been used by middle and even high school teachers of students with bigwordphobia. Of course, remedial reading teachers will need to pick and choose age-appropriate activities throughout the book.

Following Chapter Four is a short question-and-answer section. All books take a long time to write and an even longer time to get into print. This book (in its many draft stages) has been tried out with teachers, and teachers have, in turn, tried out the activities with their students. Many changes, deletions and additions to the final product derive from the savvy suggestions of these teachers and have resulted in a better book. In addition, teachers also posed questions about the role of phonics instruction in classrooms. Thus, the book ends with some of the most commonly asked questions and my attempt to answer them.

Finally, because I believe that teachers want to know the why behind the how, I have included a speech I made summarizing the research base underlying the practical activities.

1

Building the Foundation

Before we begin helping children learn letter-sound relationships they can use, we must be sure our children know what they are trying to learn and how it is useful to them. In the past decade, we have had a tremendous amount of research, usually included under the term *emergent literacy,* (Teale & Sulzby, 1991), which has shown us what happens in the homes of children where literacy is a priority. We now know that children born into homes where someone spends time with them in reading and writing activities walk into our schools with an incredible foundation upon which our instruction can easily build. These children experience an average of over 1000 hours of quality one-on-one reading and writing activities.

Parents (or parent substitutes including grandmothers, cousins, uncles, and big sisters) read to children and talk with them about what they are reading. This reading is usually done in the *lap position,* where the child can see the pictures as well as the words used to tell about the pictures. Favorite books are read time and again and eventually most children opt for a book which they *pretend-read*—usually to a younger friend or a stuffed animal.

In addition to reading, these children are exposed to writing at an early age. They scribble and make up ways to spell words. They ask (and are told) how to spell favorite words. They make words from their magnetic letters and copy favorite words from books. From the over 1000 hours of reading and writing experiences, these children learn some incredibly important concepts.

Concepts Young Children Learn from Reading-Writing Encounters

What Reading and Writing Are For

Imagine you are visiting in a first-grade classroom. You have a chance to talk with several children and ask them, "Why are you learning to read and write?" Some children answer, "You have to learn to read and write." When pushed, they can name all kinds of "real-world" products as reasons for reading and writing—books, newspapers, magazines, recipes, and maps. Other children respond to the why-learn-to-read-and-write question with answers such as, "to do your workbook," "to read in reading group," and "to go to second grade." Children who give "school-world" answers to this critical question demonstrate that they don't see reading and writing as part of their real world. Children who don't know what reading is for in the real world do not have the same drive and motivation as children for whom reading and writing, like eating and sleeping, are things everyone does. In addition, children who pretend-read a memorized book and "write" a letter to grandma are confident they can read and write!

Print Tracking and Jargon

Print is what you read and write. Print includes all the funny little marks—letters, punctuation, space between words and paragraphs—which translate into familiar spoken language. In English, we read across the page in a left-to-right fashion. Because our eyes can only see a few words during each stop (called a *fixation*), we must actually move our eyes several times to read one line of print. When we finish that line, we make a return sweep and start all over again. If there are sentences at the top of a page and a picture in the middle and more sentences at the bottom, we read the top first and then the bottom. We start at the front of a book and go toward the end.

Jargon refers to all the words we use to talk about reading and writing. Jargon includes such terms as *word, letter, sentence,* and *sound.* We use this jargon constantly as we try to teach children how to read: "Look at the first word in the second sentence. How does that word begin? What sound does that letter make?"

Using some jargon is essential to talking with children about reading and writing, but children who do not first hear this jargon at home are often hopelessly confused by it. Although all children speak in words, they don't know words exist as separate entities until they are put in the presence of reading and writing. To many children, letters are what you get in the mailbox, sounds are horns and bells and doors slamming, and sentences are what you have to serve if you get caught committing a crime! These children are unable to follow our "simple" instructions because we are using words that for them hold no meaning or an entirely different one.

Many children come into first grade knowing how to track print and knowing the jargon of print. From being read to in the lap position, they have noticed how the eyes *jump* across the lines of print as someone is reading. They have watched people write grocery lists and thank-you letters to Grandma and have observed the top-to-bottom, left-to-right movement. Often, they have typed on the computer and observed these print conventions. Because they have had someone to talk with about reading and writing, they have learned much of the jargon.

For example, while writing down a dictated thank-you note to Grandma, Dad may say, "Say your sentence one word at a time if you want me to write it. I can't write as fast as you can talk."

Or, when the child asks how to spell *birthday,* he may be told, "it starts with the letter *b,* just like your dog Buddy's name. *Birthday* and *buddy* start with the same sound and the same letter."

These children know how to look at print and what teachers are talking about as they give them information about print. All children need to develop these critical understandings in order to learn to read and write.

Phonological Awareness

Have you listened to kindergartners on the playground when they want to tease one another? What do they say? Often you hear chants, such as Billy is silly; saggy, baggy Maggie; fat Pat eats rats! Making rhymes and playing with words is one of the most reliable indicators that children are getting control of language. They are becoming aware of words and sounds and can manipulate these to express themselves—and to impress others!

This ability to manipulate sounds is called phonological awareness, and children's level of phonological awareness is very highly correlated with their success in beginning reading (Lundberg, Frost, and Petersen, 1988). Phonological awareness develops through a series of stages during which children first become aware that language is made up of individual words, that words are made up of syllables and that syllables are made up of phonemes. It is important to note here that it is not the jargon children learn. Five-year-olds cannot tell you there are three syllables in dinosaur and one syllable in Rex. What they can do is clap out the beats in dinosaur and the one beat in Rex. Likewise, they cannot tell you that the first phoneme in *mice* is *m,* but they can tell you what you would have if you took the first sound off *mice—ice.*

Children develop this phonological awareness as a result of the oral and written language they are exposed to in the preschool years. Nursery rhymes, chants, and Dr. Seuss books usually play a large role in this development. Lap reading in which children can see the print being read to them also seems to play an important role. Most children who have the luxury of being read to on demand will select a "favorite" book which they will insist on having read again and again. They will ask questions about the words: "Where does it say, 'snort'?" "Is that 'zizzerzazzerzuzz'?"

Children also develop a sense of sounds and words as they try to write. In the beginning, many children let a single letter stand for an entire word. Later, they put more letters and often say the word they want to write, dragging out its sounds to hear what letters they might use. Children who are allowed and encouraged to invent-spell develop an early and strong sense of phonological awareness.

Some Concrete Words

If you sit down with first graders on the first day of school and try to determine if they can read by giving them a simple book to read or testing them on some common words such as *the, and, of,* or *with,* you would probably conclude that most first graders can't read yet. But many first graders can read and write some words. Here are some words a boy named David knew when he began first grade:

David

Mama

Daddy

Bear Bear (his favorite stuffed animal)

Carolina (his favorite basketball team)

Pizza Hut

I love you. (Written on notes on good days.)

I hate you. (Written on notes on bad days!)

Most children who have had reading and writing experiences have learned some 10 to 15 words. The words they learn are usually concrete words important to them. This knowledge is important, not because they can read much with these few words, but because children who come to school already able to read or write some concrete words have accomplished an important and difficult task. They have learned how to learn words.

Some Letter Names and Sounds

Finally, many children have learned some letter names and sounds. They can't usually recognize all 26 letters in both upper- and lowercase and they often don't know the sounds of *w* or *c,* but they have learned the names and sounds for the most common letters. Usually, the letter names and sounds children know are based on those concrete words they can read and write.

The Foundation

Thanks to a whole decade of research on emergent literacy, we finally understand what we mean when we say a child is "not ready." We know that many children have hundreds of hours of literacy interactions during which they develop understanding critical to their success in beginning reading. We must now structure our school programs to try to provide for all children what some children have had. This will not be an easy task. We don't have 1000 hours, and we don't have the luxury of doing it with one child at a time, and when the child is interested in doing it! But we must do all we can, and we must do it in ways that are as close to the home experiences as possible. In the remainder of this chapter, I describe activities successfully used by kindergarten and first-grade teachers who are committed to putting all children in the presence of reading and writing and allowing all children to learn:

What reading and writing are for

Print tracking and jargon

Phonological awareness

Some concrete words

Some letter names and sounds

A teacher shares a predictable big book with children.

Shared Reading with Predictable Big Books

Kindergarten and first-grade teachers have always recognized the importance of reading a variety of books to children. Reading to children promotes oral language and concept development, adds to their store of information about the world, and helps them develop a sense of story. There is one particular kind of book and one particular kind of reading, however, which has special benefits for building reading and writing foundations—shared reading with predictable large-sized, or "big," books.

Shared reading is a term used to describe the process in which the teacher and the children read a book together. The book is read and reread many times. On the first several readings, the teacher does most of the reading. As the children become more familiar with the book, they join in and "share" the reading.

Predictable books are books in which repeated patterns, refrains, pictures, and rhyme allow children to pretend-read a book which has been read to them several times. Pretend reading is a stage most children go through with a favorite book which some patient adult has read and reread to them. Shared reading of predictable books allows all children to experience this pretend reading. From this pretend reading, they learn what reading is, and they develop the confidence that they will be able to do it.

Children share the
big books with one
another.

When children are read to in the lap position, they have the opportunity
to observe the print and the eyes of the person reading. They notice that the
reader always reads the top print first, then the bottom print. They notice
the reader's eyes moving from left to right and then making the return
sweep at the end of the line. children who can see the words of a favorite
book as that book is being read notice that some words occur again and
again and eventually come to recognize some of these words. As they learn
words, they notice recurring letter-sound relationships. Big books in which
the print is enlarged allow a whole class of children to get some of the ad-
vantages of lap reading. Currently, there is a great number of such books
from which to choose.

In choosing a book for shared reading in a kindergarten or first-grade
class, I have three criteria. First, the book must be very predictable. My
most important goal for shared reading is that even children with no literacy
background will be able to pretend-read the book after several readings and
develop the confidence that goes along with that accomplishment. Thus, I
want a book without too much print, and one in which the sentence patterns
are very repetitive and in which the pictures support those sentence patterns.

Second, I want a book that will be very appealing to the children. Since
the whole class of children will work with the same big book, I try to
choose a book that many children will fall in love with.

Finally, the book must "take us someplace" conceptually. Most teachers
spend several weeks with one big book. In addition to reading, rereading,
acting out the book, and numerous other activities, they build units around
the book theme and extend the children's knowledge with other books (of
normal size and not predictable).

In doing shared reading with big, predictable books, we have multiple goals. First, however, we focus on the book itself, on enjoying it, rereading it, and acting it out. As we do this, we develop concepts and oral language. When most of the children can pretend-read the book, we focus their attention on the print. Children learn print conventions and jargon and concrete words. When children know some concrete words, we use these words to begin to build some letter-sound knowledge.

To illustrate the many activities you might do with a predictable big book, I will describe activities teachers have done using the big book *Ten Little Bears* (M. Ruwe, Scott, Foresman, 1988). But first, a brief description of the book will be helpful. The opening page of *Ten Little Bears* shows ten bears of various colors and sizes sitting around a living room looking extremely bored. The text on the first two pages reads:

Ten little bears were sitting at home.

They wanted something to do.

On the following page, you see a very amused-looking bear joyously riding a sailboat on a pond. The text reads:

One little bear went for a ride in a sailboat.

The picture on page four shows nine of the original ten bears in their same bored positions. The text reads:

Then nine little bears were left at home.

Pages five and six continue the pattern established:

One little bear went for a ride in a car.

Then eight little bears were left at home.

In the following pages the pattern continues as one by one, the bears ride off in a truck, in a helicopter, on a tractor, in a moving van, on a train, in a jet, and in a fire truck. Finally,

Then one little bear was left at home.

He was fast asleep.

Soon nine little bears came home.

Then one little bear woke up.

He said, "Let's go to the park to play."

Nine little bears said, "No, let's eat."

A teacher doing a first-time reading of *Ten Little Bears.*

Ten Little Bears offers many opportunities for concept development. It can be part of a unit on vehicles or a unit on travel. Number concepts can be developed as each bear leaves, leaving one fewer bored bear. The following are some of the activities teachers have used (Cunningham and Allington, 1991).

Read and Talk About the Book

Parents who read to their children not only read but also engage the children in conversation about the book and reread favorite books. We try to promote this kind of conversation and interaction as each book is read. After reading the first two pages ("Ten little bears were sitting at home. They wanted something to do."), the teacher would encourage predictions by asking, "What do you think they might do?" Children would be encouraged to infer character feelings by responding to questions, such as "How are these bears feeling?"

They relate their own experience to the book by responding to "Have you ever been bored? What do you do when you are bored?"

As the book continues and it becomes apparent that each bear is going to go for a ride in some kind of vehicle, children are asked to predict which bear they think is going next and what kind of a vehicle that bear will ride in. Finally, only one bear is left (the sleeping bear). The teacher encourages thinking, language, and book engagement by asking questions: "What will this bear want to do when he wakes up? Why do you think the sleeping bear wants to go to the park to play and all the other bears want to eat?"

**Children acting out
Ten Little Bears.**

Act Out the Book

Prepare for this activity by making cards that designate which bear is which. The simplest procedure is to make a simple line drawing of each of the vehicles on construction paper, writing the word (sailboat, car, etc.) on the back of the paper. For the last bear, who doesn't ride in a vehicle, draw a sleeping bear. Punch two holes and put yarn through so that children can wear the cards around their necks. Laminate these so you can use them again and again.

Distribute the cards to ten children and let them come up and sit around on the floor looking very bored. Reread the book, letting the appropriate children go off to ride in their vehicle. Letting the children make vehicle noises as they ride adds to the fun of this activity. Before you turn each page, ask the children who are watching, "Which little bear is going next?" Count after each bear leaves to see how many are left and then let the children help you read the refrains—"Then seven little bears were left at home."

Act out the book enough times so that each child has a chance to be one of the little bears. You may want to leave the book and the laminated cards in a center so that children can act out and read the book again and again.

Record Children "Reading" the Book

Let the children help you make an audio tape of the book. You may want to read some pages and designate certain children to read the pages that tell what each bear rides off in. Let the whole group read the refrain pages that tell how many bears were left at home. Put this tape in a listening center so that children can listen to themselves reading!

Learn More About Vehicles

Let the children help you reread the book and list all the vehicles on the board. You may want to make a web that shows certain categories (land, sea, and air, perhaps). Lead children to name other vehicles and add these to the web. Have children describe the vehicles and tell what they are used for. Read them some informational books about vehicles. Have them find pictures of vehicles and make a collage bulletin board. You may want to have a "Bring Your Vehicles Day" on which children bring their favorite little cars, trucks, and airplanes. Be sure to compare and contrast the vehicles brought and use them in a writing activity.

Study and Compare Real and Fictional Bears

Reread the book and ask the children questions which will help them understand the differences between real bears and storybook bears: "Do real bears live in houses? Where do real bears live?" Read them some informational books about real bears and help them understand the difference between fantasy and informational text. You may want to have a "Bring Your Bear Day."

Count Forward and Backward

Reread the book, counting the bears on each page. Use the book to help children understand that counting is adding one at a time and counting backwards is taking one away.

Let Children Be the Words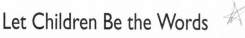

In Being the Words, children are given the words and they come up and make the sentences. They do this by matching their word to the words in the book. Two pages of the book are matched at a time. To prepare for this activity, write all the words on sentence strips and cut them to match the size

Children "being the words" to make the sentences from the book.

of the word. Do not make duplicate words unless they are needed to make the sentences on the two pages of the book which will be displayed simultaneously. Do make separate cards for any words which are sometimes shown with a capital letter and sometimes used with a small letter. Make separate cards for each punctuation mark needed. Laminate these cards so that you can use them over and over.

Begin the activity by passing out all the cards containing the words and punctuation marks. Let the children look at their words and point out the distinction between words and punctuation marks. Tell the children that they are going to be their words and come up and make the sentences in the book.

Open the book to display the first two pages. Ask the children to read the sentences with you:

> **Ten little bears were sitting at home.**
> **They wanted something to do.**

Point to each word as you reread the sentences and have the children look to see if their word matches any of the words they see in the book. Explain that you don't say anything when you get to the period but that it lets you know the sentence is over. Have all the children who have a word or punctuation mark in this sentence come up and get in the right order to make the sentence. Help the children to arrange themselves in the appropriate left-to-right order, to get the periods at the end of the sentences, and to hold the words right side up. When everyone is in order, have the children not in the sentence read the sentence as you move behind each child who is a word.

Have all the words sit down, display the next two pages and have them read from the book:

> **One little bear went for a ride in a sailboat.**
> **Then nine little bears were left at home.**

Children sorting the words of *Ten Little Bears* according to the number of letters.

Again, have the children come up and arrange themselves. Let the children sitting down read the sentences from the word cards as you walk behind each word. Continue until children have made all the sentences in the book.

Being the Words is one of the favorite activities of most children, and they ask to do it again and again. Through this activity, children learn what words are, that words make up sentences, that punctuation signals the end of the sentence but is not read. They also practice the left-to-right order of print and realize that the order the words are in makes a difference in what you read. Some children also learn many of the words during this activity. You will observe this as you give out the words to do the activity a second or third time and hear children say things like, "Oh, boy, I'm the helicopter!"

Many teachers put the book and the laminated words in a center. Children delight in turning the pages of the book and laying out the words on the floor to make the sentences.

Sort Words According to Length

Sorting the words is another activity that uses the laminated word cards made for Being the Words. Again distribute all the words to the children (excluding duplicates and punctuation marks). Tell the children that they are going to help you sort the words according to how many letters they have. Write the numeral *1* on the blackboard or on a piece of paper and ask all children who have a word with just one letter in it to come up. The child with the word *a* should come up. Place this word along the blackboard's chalk ledge under the *1*. Continue with words that have two letters—*at, to, do, in, on, he, up, go, No*—then three letters, and so on until you get the ten-letter word *helicopter.* Put all the words on the chalk ledge under the appropriate numeral. When all the words are in the right place, have the children guess which number has the most words. Let them help you count each group and write the total number of words found under the numeral. After doing this activity with the whole class, many teachers put the numeral cards and word cards in a center and have children work with a partner to sort them.

Sorting the words according to length is a good activity to integrate reading and math. It also helps children become clear about the distinction between words and letters and helps them learn to focus on the individual letters in words. In addition, you can compare the words and help the children learn such jargon as long, short, longer, shorter, longest, shortest.

Use Pocket Chart and Hide Words

The idea of using a pocket chart and hiding the words was adapted from one suggested by the McCrackens in their wonderful book *Songs, Stories and Poetry to Teach Reading and Writing* (1988). Write the sentences from several of the pages on sentence strips. Read the sentences with the children and then let the children watch as you cut the sentences into words and place them in a pocket chart. Choose a child to be "it." Let this child come and, while the other children have their eyes closed, turn over one of the word cards so that the word is hidden. Give an "open eyes" signal, and let the children reread to try to figure out what the hidden word is. Let the child who hid the word pick another child to guess the hidden word. If guessed correctly, let the child who guessed turn the hidden word back over. Repeat this procedure by letting the child who guessed correctly hide another word. This is another activity children like to do together in centers.

Let Children Make a "Ten Little Bears" Book

Make photocopy masters on which are written traceable words; the children can use them as pages in making their own "Ten Little Bears" book. You may want to include simple drawings for the children to color or let them draw pictures for each page. Give out one page (front and back) of the book each day. Have the children trace and read the words and color or draw appropriate pictures. Collect the pages and keep them until the entire book can be made. Let each child make and decorate a book cover and put together their own book to take home.

Write Simple Texts Using Words and Pictures

Using a pocket chart, chart paper, chalkboard, or photocopy master, use the vocabulary from the book, any other words the children know, and rebus pictures to create some new sentences, poems, or stories for them to read. Here are some of the possibilities created by teachers using the *Ten Little Bears* vocabulary. The following is sung to the tune of *Ten Little Indians*. This song also works with sailboats, tractors, fire trucks, and moving vans:

One little, two little, three little helicopters,

Four little, five little, six little helicopters,

Seven little, eight little, nine little helicopters,

Ten little helicopters go.

The next example uses pictures for the animal words and assumes known color words or a color word chart. Numbers are done on separate pages and go to ten:

One cat.

One little cat.

One little black cat.

One little black cat in a car.

Two dogs.

Two little dogs.

Two little white dogs.

Two little white dogs in a helicopter.

Last is the *Ten Little Bears* story rewritten with big boys (or girls) substituted for little bears and places for vehicles. It can be made into a book for the children to illustrate or can be written on a chart and acted out by the children:

Ten big boys were sitting at home.

They wanted something to do.

One big boy went to the zoo.

Then nine big boys were left at home.

One big boy went to the grocery store.

Then eight big boys were left at home.

The boys go on to the toy store, the baseball field, the library, the mall, the pet store, the park, and the museum. The story ends in a similar way to the *Ten Little Bears.*

Then one big boy was left at home.

He was fast asleep.

Soon nine big boys came home.

Then one big boy woke up.

He said, "Let's play something."

Nine big boys said, "No, let's eat."

Sort Words According to Letters

Pass out to the children all the laminated words used in Being the Words. Tape a long strip of butcher paper across the chalkboard. Draw lines and divide it into 26 bars, labeled *A* to *Z* (both capital and small). Beginning with *A,* go through each letter of the alphabet, letting all the children whose word contains that letter come up front. Once all the children are up there, have each child make a tally mark in the appropriate letter bar. (If a word has two of the designated letter, that child should make two tally marks.) Count the tally marks and write the total number. Have the children with the words containing the letter *a* sit down and go on with the *b*'s, *c*'s, and so on. Children are generally amazed to see that there are 27 *t*'s and 33 *e*'s! They are disappointed to discover that there is not a single *z* in the entire book!

Sorting the letters takes some time, but the children love to do it and become much more aware of the individual letters in words. (One child in a kindergarten excitedly announced that *Zak,* his name, had a *z!* Another child brought to school the next day a Pizza Hut advertisement to show there were *z*'s in words!) Sorting the letters is a good math activity, also. Some teachers, instead of simple tally marks, have the children color in bars to indicate the designated letter. The *e* bar is colored in almost to the top, whereas the *z* bar has no coloring at all. Graphs allow the children to *graphically* see the number relationships.

Sort Words for Just One Letter

With the sorting activity you can help the children focus their attention on just one letter. The *t,* for example, occurs in 24 of the words. To do this activity, you would pass out only those words that contain the letter *t.* Have children come up and display their word in response to questions, such as which words have:

T **as the first letter (ten, two, three, they, to, then, truck, tractor, train, the)?**

T **as the last letter (eight, at, went, left, fast, sailboat, jet, eat)?**

T **somewhere in the word but not first or last (little, sitting, wanted, something, helicopter, tractor, let's)?**

Two t's in the word (sitting, tractor)?

T **with an h after it (three, they, something, then, the)?**

T **with an r after it (truck, tractor, train)?**

In addition to sorting words according to where the letters appear, the words can be sorted according to the sound children hear. Tell the children that *t* usually has the sound you hear at the beginning of *ten,* the end of *jet,* and in the middle of *tractor.* Have the children who have the words *ten, jet,* and *tractor* come and stand on one side of you. Tell the children that sometimes *t* has other sounds, as in the word *three.* Have the child with the word *three* come and stand on the other side of you. Then have all the children bring their words and decide by listening whether the *t* has the sound in *ten, jet,* and *tractor* or another sound and stand on the appropriate side. Conclude the lesson by having the children count the words on the *ten, jet, tractor* side and on the *three* side. Help them to generalize that *t* usually has the sound you hear in *ten, jet,* and *tractor* but that it can have other sounds.

Use Words as Key Words

Letter sounds, like other information, can be learned by rote or by association. Learning the common sound for *b* by trying to remember it, or by trying to remember that it begins the word *bears* when you can't read the word itself, requires rote learning. Once you can read the word *bears* and realize that the common sound for *b* is heard at the beginning of the word, you no longer have to just remember the sound. You can now associate the sound of *b* with something already known, the word *bears.* Associative learning is the easiest, quickest and most long lasting.

Children from print-rich environments know some concrete words when they come to school. As they are taught letter sounds, they probably associate these with the words they know, thus making the learning of these sounds easier and longer lasting. We can provide this opportunity for associative learning to children who did not know words when they came to school by capitalizing on the words they have learned from *Ten Little Bears.*

The number of letter sounds you wish to focus on from one book will depend on what your children already know. If their knowledge of beginning sounds is minimal, you may only want to teach five or six sounds using clear, concrete key words with pure initial sounds; but use words most of the children have learned. The words *bear, car, five, go, helicopter, jet, little, no, park, ride, sailboat, ten,* and *van* have clear initial sounds and are apt to be learned easily by most children because they are repeated often or because they are "exciting" words.

Regardless of how many letter sounds you teach using the *Ten Little Bears* key words, the procedure should be the same. Begin with two letters which are very different in look and sound and which are made in different places in the mouth—*b* and *l,* for example. Show the children the two words—*bear* and *little*—which will serve as key words for these letters. Have the children pronounce the two key words, and notice the position of their tongue and teeth as they do. Have one child stand in the front of the room and hold the word *bear.* Have another child hold the word *little.* Say several concrete words (*bike, lemon, box, book, ladder, lady, boy*) which begin like *bear* or *little* and have the children say them after you. Have them notice where their tongue and teeth are as they say the words. Let the children point to the child holding *bear* or *little* to indicate how the word begins.

Begin a key-word bulletin board on which you put the letters *b* and *l* and the key words *bear* and *little.* Repeat the activity just described using other *b* and *l* words until most of the children begin to understand the difference in the sounds of the letters. Then add a third letter and key word—perhaps *n* and *no.* Have them listen for and repeat words beginning with all three letters—*b, l, n.* Be sure to point out that the words they already know will help them remember the sound.

Teach Blending with Rhyming Words

Children from print-rich environments often infer a decoding principle based on the words they read. They notice that words, such as *fish, wish, dish* and *hop, pop, stop* sound alike and look alike. Teaching children to blend beginning sounds they know to make rhyming words gives them some early decoding ability.

The easiest words with which to teach this blending-rhyming principle are words to which you can add letters to make new words. In *Ten Little Bears,* there are four such words—*at, in, up,* and *eat.* To teach this lesson, put a word such as *at* on the board. Tell children that by blending some of the beginning sounds they know with *at,* they can make lots of new words.

Use only those initial letters for which you have taught a sound, and if you have a bulletin board of key words for the initial sound, remind children to look at it to help them remember the sound for the first letters. Under the word *at,* write *at* again and then add a letter to "magically" change *at* to a new word. Let children read each new word and talk about what it means.

Writing

Until recently, writing in kindergarten and first-grade classrooms referred to handwriting instruction. Children were not usually allowed or encouraged to write until they could make most of the letters correctly and spell lots of words. The theory was that if children were allowed to write before they could spell and make the letters correctly, they would acquire "bad habits" that later would be hard to break. There is a certain logic in this argument, but this logic does not hold up to scrutiny when you actually look at children before they come to school.

Just as children from literacy-oriented homes read before they can read by pretend-reading a memorized book, they write before they can write! Their writing is usually not readable by anyone besides them, and sometimes they read the same scribbling different ways. They write with pens, markers, crayons, paint, chalk, and with normal-sized pencils with erasers on the ends! They write on chalkboards, magic slates, walls, drawing paper, and lined notebook paper. (They just ignore the lines!)

They write in scribbles, which first go anywhere and then show a definite left-to-right orientation. They make letterlike forms. They underline certain letters to show word boundaries. As they learn more about words and letters, they let single letters stand for entire words. They draw pictures and intersperse letters with the pictures. They make grocery lists by copying words off packages. They copy favorite words from books. They write love letters (I love you Mama) and hate mail (I hate you Mama).

Emergent literacy research has shown us that children are not ruined by being allowed to write before they can write. Rather, they learn many important concepts and develop the confidence that they can write (Sulzby, Teale, and Kamberelis, 1989). Here are some activities that promote writing for all.

Let Children Watch You Write

As children watch you write, they observe that you always start in a certain place, go in certain directions and leave space between words. In addition to these print conventions, they observe that writing is "talk written down." There are numerous opportunities in every classroom for the teacher to write as the children watch—and sometimes help—with suggestions of what to write.

Language experience is a time-honored practice in which the teacher records the children's ideas. Language experience can take the form of a group-dictated chart, which may list what the class learned about monkeys, or an individually dictated sentence recorded at the bottom of a child's picture. Language experience takes place whenever a child's words are recorded so the child can see that writing is truly a permanent record of speech.

In many classrooms, the teacher begins the day by writing a morning message on the board. The teacher writes this short message as the children watch. The teacher then reads the message, pointing to each word and inviting the children to join in on any words they know. Sometimes, teachers take a few minutes to point out some things students might notice from the morning message:

How many sentences did I write today?

How can we tell how many there are?

What do we call this mark I put at the end of this sentence?

Do we have any words that begin with the same letters?

Which is the longest word?

These and similar questions help children learn print tracking and jargon and focus their attention on words and letters.

Often, teachers write things that are connected to the books they are reading with the children. In the shared reading description about the *Ten Little Bears,* the teacher helps the children to compose the *Ten Little Helicopters* and the *Ten Big Boys* and then writes these for the children to see.

Class books are another opportunity for children to watch teachers write. During a unit on nutrition, children told their favorite vegetables. The teacher recorded each child's favorites on one page, which that child illustrated. The pages were bound together into a class book on *Vegetables We Like,* which was put into the reading center and remained a very popular reading choice.

First graders
illustrating their
"published" books.

Provide Variety in Writing Utensils and Surfaces

Children like a variety of things to write with and on. They view writing as a "creation" and are often motivated to write by various media. Many teachers (packrats, by nature) find outrageous purple stationery in the "ten cents" bin of the local bargain store; pick up any and all free postcards, scratch pads, counter checks, pens, and pencils; and haunt yard sales, always on the lookout for an extra chalkboard or an old—but still working—typewriter. A letter to parents at the beginning of the year, asking them to clean out the desk and drawers at home and donate surplus writing utensils and paper of various kinds, often brings unexpected treasures. In addition to the usual writing media, young children like to write with sticks in sand, with sponges on chalkboards and with chocolate pudding and shaving cream.

Help Children Find Writing Purposes

For most young children, the purpose of writing is to get something told or done. Encourage children to make grocery lists while they are playing in the housekeeping center, to make a birthday card for a friend or relative, to write a note to you or one of their classmates. Let them make signs (Keep Out! Girls Only!) and post them as part of their dramatic play. Let them label things and the places where those things are supposed to go.

   In most classrooms, there is a "sharing time" at some point in the day. You may encourage children to "draw and write what you want to tell us about at sharing time."

A print-rich classroom.

Provide a Print-Rich Classroom

Classrooms in which children write contain lots of print in them. In addition to books, there are magazines and newspapers. Charts of recipes tried and directions for building things hang as reminders. Children's names are on their desks and on many different objects. There are class books, bulletin boards with labeled pictures of animals under study, and labels on almost everything. Children's drawings and all kinds of writing are displayed. In these classrooms, children see that all kinds of writing is valued. Equally important, children who want to write "the grown-up way" can find lots of words to make the their own.

Accept Whatever Kind of Writing They Do

Accepting a variety of writing—from scribbling to one-letter representations, to invented spellings, to copied words—is the key to having young children write before they can write. Sometimes, it is the children and not the teacher who reject beginning attempts. If more advanced children give the less advanced children a hard time about their "scribbling," the teacher must intervene and firmly state a policy, such as:

There are many different ways to communicate through writing. We use pictures and letters and words. Sometimes we just scribble, but the scribbling helps us remember what we are thinking. We use all these different ways in this classroom!

Without this attitude of acceptance, the very children who most need to explore language through writing will be afraid to write.

In the next section, children use writing as a way to help them focus their attention on the letters in their names. When the teacher accepts whatever kind of writing they can do, the children all try to write. As they go through all the names in the classroom, the writing of all children becomes much more conventional.

Names and Other Concrete Words

Get-Acquainted Activities

Most kindergarten and first-grade teachers begin their year with some get-acquainted activities. As part of these activities, they often assign special status to a child each day. In addition to learning about each child, you can focus attention on the special child's name and use the name to develop some important understandings about words and letters (Cunningham, 1988).

To prepare for this activity, write all the children's first names (with initials for last names if two names are the same) with a permanent marker on sentence strips. Cut the strips so that long names have long strips and short names, short strips. Each day, reach into the box and draw out a name. This child becomes the "King, or Queen, for a day" and the child's name becomes the focus of many activities. Reserve a bulletin board and add each child's name to the board. (Some teachers like to have children bring a snapshot of themselves or take pictures of the children to add to the board as the names are added. Here is a day-by-day example of what you might do with children's names.

DAY ONE

Close your eyes. Reach into the box, shuffle the names around, and draw one out. Call that child forward and crown him or her king or queen for the day! Lead the other children to interview this child and find out what he or she likes to eat, play, do after school. Does he or she have brothers? Sisters?

Cats? Dogs? Mice? Some teachers record this information on an experience chart or compile a class book, with one page of information about each child.

Now focus the children's attention on the child's name, for example, David. Point to the word *David* on the sentence strip and develop children's understanding of jargon by pointing out that this **word** is David's name. Tell them that it takes many **letters** to write the word *David* and let them help you count the letters. Say the letters in David—D-a-v-i-d—and have the children chant them with you. Point out that the word *David* **begins** and **ends** with the **same** letter. Explain that the *d* looks different because one is a **capital** D and the other is a **small** d (or, **uppercase/lowercase,** whatever jargon you use).

Take another sentence strip and have children watch as you write *David.* Have them chant the spelling of the letters with you. Cut the letters apart and mix them up. Let several children come and arrange the letters in just the right order so that they spell *David.* Have the other children chant to check that the order is correct.

Give each child a large sheet of drawing paper and, using crayons, have them write *David* in large letters on one side of the paper. Model at the board how to write each letter as they write it. Do not worry if what they write is not perfect (or even doesn't bear much resemblance to the one you wrote) and resist the temptation to correct what they wrote. Remember that children who write at home before entering school often reverse letters and make them in funny ways. The important understanding is that names are words, that words can be written, and that it takes lots of letters to write them.

Finally, have everyone draw a picture of David on the other side of the drawing paper. Let David take all the pictures home!

DAY TWO

Draw another name—say, *Catherine.* Crown Catherine and do for her whatever interviewing and chart making you did for David. (Decide carefully what you will do for the first children because every child will expect equal treatment!)

Focus their attention on Catherine's name. Say the letters in Catherine and have the children chant them with you. Help the children count the letters and decide which letter is **first, last,** and so on. Point out that Catherine has two *e*'s and they look exactly the same because they are both small (lowercase) *e*'s. Write *Catherine* on another sentence strip and cut it up into letters. Have children arrange the letters to spell *Catherine,* using the name in the first sentence strip as their model.

Put *Catherine* on the bulletin board under *David* and compare the two. Which has more letters? How many more letters are in the word *Catherine* than in the word *David?* Does *Catherine* have any of the same letters as *David?*

Finish the lesson by having everyone write *Catherine.* Have everyone draw pictures for Catherine and let her take them all home.

DAY THREE

Draw the third name—*Debbie.* Do the crowning, interviewing and chart making. Chant the letters in Debbie's name. Write it again, cut it up, and do the letter arranging. Be sure to note the two *e*'s and two *b*'s and to talk about first and last letters.

As you put *Debbie* on the bulletin board, compare it to both *David* and *Catherine.* This is a perfect time to notice that both *David* and *Debbie* begin with the same letter and the same sound. Finish the lesson by having the children write *Debbie* and draw pictures for Debbie to take home.

DAY FOUR

Mike comes out. Do all the usual activities. When you put *Mike* on the bulletin board, help children to realize that David has lost the dubious distinction of having the shortest name. (Zeb may now look down at the name card on his desk and call out that his name is even shorter. You will point out that he is right but that Mike's name is the shortest one on the bulletin board right now. What is really fascinating about this activity is how the children compare their own names to the ones on the board even before their names get there. That is exactly the kind of word-letter awareness you are trying to develop!)

When you have a one-syllable name with which there are many rhymes (*Pat, Tran, Joe, Sue,* etc.), seize the opportunity to help the children listen for words that rhyme with that name. Say pairs of words—some of which rhyme with Mike (Mike/ball, Mike/bike, Mike/hike, Mike/cook, Mike/like). If the pairs rhyme, everyone should point at Mike and shout "MIKE." If not, they should shake their heads and frown.

DAY FIVE

Cynthia comes out. Do the various activities, and then take advantage of the fact that the names *Catherine* and *Cynthia* both begin with the letter *c* but begin with different sounds.

Have Catherine and Cynthia stand on opposite sides of you. Write their names above them on the chalkboard. Have the children say *Catherine* and *Cynthia* several times—drawing out the first sound. Help them to understand that some letters can have more than one sound and that the names *Catherine* and *Cynthia* show us that. Tell the class that you are going to say some words, all of which begin with the letter *c*. Some of these words sound like *Catherine* at the beginning and some of them sound like *Cynthia*. Say some words and have the children say them with you (*cat, celery, candy, cookies, city, cereal, cut*). For each word, have them point to Catherine or Cynthia in order to show which sound they hear. Once they have decided, write each word under *Catherine* or *Cynthia*.

DAY SIX TO DAY LAST

Continue featuring a special child each day. For each child, do the standard interviewing, charting, chanting, letter arranging, writing, drawing activities. Then, take advantage of the names you have in helping children develop understanding about how letters and sound work. The following are some extra activities many teachers do with names.

Write the letters of the alphabet across the board. Count to see how many names contain each letter. Make tally marks or a bar graph and decide which letters are included in the most names and which letters are in the fewest names. Are there any letters which no one in the whole class has in his or her name?

Make up riddles about the children's names. (This is a girl. She has six letters in her name. She has two *e*'s and two *b*'s). Let the children make up riddles.

Pass out laminated letter cards—one letter to a card, lowercase on one side and uppercase on the other. Call out a name from the bulletin board and lead the children to chant the letters in the name. Then, let the children who have those letters come up and display the letters and lead the class in a chant—cheerleader style. "David, D-a-v-i-d, David—Yeh! Yeh!"

Letter Names and Sounds Activities

Shared reading, writing, and learning concrete words such as names are all activities through which children learn many letter names and sounds. There are, however, other activities which children enjoy and which speed up their letter and sound knowledge.

Sing the Alphabet Song and Read Alphabet Books

The Alphabet Song has been sung to the tune of *Twinkle, Twinkle Little Star* by generations of children. Children enjoy it and it does seem to give them a sense of all the letters and a framework in which to put new letters as they learn them. Many children come to school already able to sing *The Alphabet Song.* Let them sing it and teach it to everyone else. Once the children can sing the song, you may want to point as they sing to alphabet cards (usually found above the chalkboard). Children enjoy "being the alphabet" as they line up to go somewhere. Simply pass your laminated alphabet cards—one to each child, leftovers go to the teacher—and let the children sing the song slowly as each child lines up. Be sure to hand out the cards randomly so that no one gets to be the A and lead the line or has to be the Z and bring up the rear every day!

There are some wonderful alphabet books which not only teach the letters but help children develop concepts. Here are just a few of my favorites. There are many more. Once you and the children have read several alphabet books, make a class alphabet book:

26 Letters and 99 Cents (Tana Hoban; Greenwillow, 1987)

ABC's: The American Indian Way (R. Red Hawk; Sierra Oaks, 1988)

A, My Name Is Alice (J. Bayer; Dial, 1986)

Alison's Zinnia (Anita Lobel; Greenwillow, 1990)

Alphabetics (Suse Macdonald; Bradbury Press, 1986)

Animalia (G. Base; Abrams, 1986)

Animals, A–Z (David McPhail; Scholastic, 1993)

Anno's Alphabet (Mitsumas Anno; Crowell, 1975)

Ashanti to Zulu: African Traditions (Margaret Musgrove; Dial Books, 1976)

Bruno Munari's ABC (Bruno Munari; World, 1960)

Easy as Pie (Marcia and Michael Folsom, Clarion, 1985)

Eating the Alphabet: Fruits and Vegetables from A–Z (Lois Short; Harcourt, Brace, Jovanovich, 1982)

Gretchen's ABC (G. D. Simpson; HarperCollins, 1991)

Harold's ABC (Crocket Johnson; HarperCollins, 1981)

Hosie's Alphabet (Hosea Tobias and Lisa Baskin; Viking Press, 1972)

Q Is for Duck (Mary Elting and Michael Folsom; Clarion, 1980)

The ABC Bunny (Wanda Gag; Coward-McCann, 1933)

The Calypso Alphabet (J. Agard; Henry Holt, 1989)

The Dinosaur Alphabet Book, The Ocean Alphabet Book, The Icky Bug Alphabet Book and all the others in the series (Jerry Pallotta; Charlesbridge, 1991)

The Handmade Alphabet (L. Rankin; Dial, 1991)

The Sesame Street ABC Book of Words (Harry McNaught; Random House/ Children's Television Workshop, 1988)

The Z Was Zapped: A Play in 26 Acts (Chris Van Allsburg; Houghton Mifflin, 1987)

Do Letter Actions

Teach children actions for the consonants. Write the letter on one side of a large index card and the action on the other. The first time you teach each letter, make a big deal of it. Get out the rhythm sticks and the marching music when you march. Go out on the playground and jump rope and do jumping jacks. Play hopscotch and pretend to be bunnies.

Once the children have learned actions for several letters, there are many activities you can do right in the classroom without any props. Have all the children stand by their desks and wait until you show them a letter. They should do that action until you hide that letter behind your back. When they have all stopped and you have their attention again, show them another letter and have them do that action. Continue this with as many letters as you have time to fill. Be sure to make comments, such as, "Yes, I see everyone marching because *M* is our marching letter."

In another activity, you pass out the letters for which children have learned actions to individual children. Each child gets up and does the action required and calls on someone to guess which letter that child was given.

In "Follow the Letter Leader," the leader picks a letter card and does that action. Everyone else follows the leader doing the same action. The leader then picks another card, and the game continues.

Teachers have different favorite actions, and you will have your own favorites. Try to pick actions with which everyone is familiar and which are called by only one name. Here is a list of actions I like. The action for *s* is my particular favorite. You can use it to end the game. Children say, "It is not an action at all"; but they remember that "s is the sitting letter":

bounce	kick	talk
catch	laugh	vacuum
dance	march	walk
fall	nod	yawn
gallop	paint	zip
hop	run	
jump	sit	

Associate Letters with Foods

Children remember what they do and what they eat. Many teachers like to feature a food when they are studying a particular letter. Children help to prepare the food and then eat it. Try to pick nutritious foods which children like; although even the children who hated zucchini remembered it was their *z* food! When they complained, their teacher asked, "What food do

Children doing the letter actions, *yawn* for *y* and *hop* for *h*.

you like that begins with *z*?" Later, a child brought zucchini bread which was a hit with most. Some possible foods:

bananas	Kool-aid	toast
cookies	lemonade	vegetables
donuts	milk	watermelon
fish	noodles	yogurt
gum	pizza	zucchini bread
hamburgers	raisins	
jello	soup	

Print Tracking—My First Book About Me

Some children have a great deal of difficulty learning to track print. In spite of the shared reading and writing activities they participate in, they don't learn how you must move from left to right and top to bottom. Often, these are the same children who don't learn any of the concrete words included in the shared-reading and shared-writing stories. These children can learn to track print and some concrete words with some focused individual language experience activities. Here is what one teacher does with the one or two children each year who don't learn to track print and/or don't learn any words from the group activities.

DAY ONE

1. Sit down with the individual child and begin a book. Explain to the child that he or she is going to make a book about himself or herself. Talk with the child and decide on one sentence to go on the first page. Try to have a long enough sentence so that it takes two lines to write. Write that sentence as the child watches.

    Ebony is in the first grade at Clemmons School.

2. Help the child read the sentence by moving her hand under each word. Read it together, pointing to each word until the child can read it and point to the words by herself.

3. As the child watches and says the individual words, write the sentence again on a sentence strip. Have the child read the sentence on the strip, pointing to each word.

4. As the child watches, cut the sentence from the strip into words. Mix these words up and have the child put the words in order to make the sentence, using the sentence in the book to match to.

5. Put the cut-up words in an envelope, and label the envelope and the page of the book with a *1*.

6. Let the child draw a picture to illustrate page one of the book.

DAY TWO

1. Reread the sentence on page one. Take the words from the envelope and put them in order by matching to the book sentence.

2. Together, compose another sentence about the child for page two. Write that sentence as the child watches.

> Ebony comes to school on Bus 19.

3. Have the child read the sentence with you several times, helping her point to words while reading them.

4. Write this sentence on a strip, cut it apart, have it matched to the book sentence, and put it in an envelope labeled *2*. Let the child illustrate page two of her book.

DAY THREE

1. Reread the sentences on pages one and two. Take the words from the envelope and put them in order by matching to both sentences.

2. Have the child find any duplicate words and decide that they are the same word and what that word is. In our example, the words *Ebony* and *school* are repeated.

3. Come up with a third sentence for page three. Use the same procedures of writing this sentence on the sentence strip, cutting, matching, and illustrating as were used for pages one and two.

> Ebony likes to eat pizza and apple pie.

DAY FOUR TO BOOK COMPLETION

Continue adding a page each day, matching the words and looking for repeated words. Read the whole book each day but when you have five or more pages, don't match all the preceding pages, but just the two or three most recent ones. Look for duplicate words and observe which ones the child is learning. When the book is finished, have the child read the whole book and ask the child to find words from the envelopes that she can read. Most children learn to track print and accumulate eight to ten words through doing one 12- to 15-page book. Some children need to do a second book, using the same procedure.

Phonological Awareness

Many of the activities discussed previously in this chapter help children develop phonological awareness. As they participate in shared reading and writing, they become aware of words as separate entities. Being the Words, cutting sentences into words and rearranging them, making new sentences from familiar words—all help children understand what words are. Encouraging invented spelling is one of the main ways teachers have of helping children develop their understanding of how phonemes make up words. As children try to spell words, they say them slowly, listening to themselves saying the sounds and thinking about what they are learning about letters and sounds. Following are other activities you can use to promote phonological awareness.

Count Words

To count words, all children should have ten counters in a paper cup. (Anything manipulable is fine. Some teachers use edibles such as raisins, grapes, or small crackers and let the children eat their counters at the end of the lesson. This makes clean-up quick and easy!) Begin by counting some familiar objects in the room (windows, doors, trash cans, etc.), having all children place one of their counters on their desks as each object is pointed to. Have children return counters to the cup before beginning to count each object.

Tell children that you can also count words by putting down a counter for each word you say. Explain that you will say a sentence in the normal way and then repeat the sentence, pausing after each word. The children should put down counters as you slowly say the words in the sentence, and then count the counters and decide how many words you said. As usual, children's attention is better if you make sentences about them. (Carol has a big smile. Paul is back at school today. I saw Jack at church.) Once the children catch on to the activity, let them say some sentences, first in the normal way, then one word at a time. Listen carefully as they say their sentences the first time because they will often need help saying them one word at a time. Children enjoy this activity, and not only are they learning to separate out words in speech, they are also practicing critical counting skills!

Clap Syllables

Once children can automatically separate the speech stream into words, they are ready to begin thinking about separating words into some components. The first division most children learn to make is that of syllables.

Clapping seems the easiest way to get every child involved, and the children's names (what else?) are the naturally appealing words to clap. Say the first name of one child. Say the name again, and this time, clap the syllables. Continue saying first names and then clapping the syllables as you say them the second time and invite the children to join in clapping with you. As children catch on, say some ███████ names. The term *syllables* is a little jargony and foreign to most young children, so you may want to refer to the syllables as beats. Children should realize by clapping that *Paul* is a one-beat word, *Miguel,* a two-beat word, and *Madeira* is a three-beat word.

Once children can clap syllables and decide how many beats a given word has, help them to see that one-beat words are usually shorter than three beat words—that is, they take fewer letters to write. To do this, write on sentence strips some words children cannot read and cut the strips into words so that short words have short strips and long words have long strips. Have some of the words begin with the same letters but be different lengths so that children will need to think about word length to decide which word is which.

For the category *animals,* you might write horse and hippopotamus; dog and donkey; kid and kangaroo; and rat, rabbit, and rhinoceros. Tell the children that you are going to say the names of animals and they should clap to show how many beats the word has. (Do not show them the words yet!) Say the first pair, one at a time (horse/hippopotamus). Help children to decide that horse is a one-beat word and hippopotamus takes a lot more claps and is a five-beat word. Now, show them the two words and say, "One of these words is horse and the other is hippopotamus. Who thinks they can figure out which one is horse and which one is hippopotamus?" Help the children by explaining that because hippopotamus takes so many beats to say it, it probably takes more letters to write it. Continue with other pairs—and finally with a triplet, to challenge your stars!

Work with Nursery Rhymes

One of the best indicators of how well children will learn to read is their ability to recite nursery rhymes when they walk into the kindergarten! Since this is such a reliable indicator, and since rhymes are so naturally appealing to children at this age, kindergarten classrooms should be filled with rhymes. Children should learn to recite these rhymes, should sing the rhymes, should clap to the rhymes, act out the rhymes, and pantomime the rhymes. In some kindergarten classrooms, they develop "raps" for the rhymes.

Once the children can recite many rhymes, nursery rhymes can be used to teach the concept of rhyme. The class can be divided into two halves—one half says the rhyme but stops when they get to the last rhyming word. The other half waits to shout the rhyme at the appropriate moment:

FIRST HALF: There was an old woman who lived in a shoe. She had so many children, she didn't know what to
SECOND HALF: do
FIRST HALF: She gave the ████████ ithout any bread and spanked them all soundly and put them to
SECOND HALF: bed.

Children also enjoy making rhymes really silly by making up a new word that rhymes:

Jack be nimble. Jack be quick.
Jack jump over Pat and Dick!

Nursery and other rhymes have been a part of our oral heritage for generations. Now we know that the rhythm and rhyme inherent in nursery rhymes are important vehicles for the beginning development of phonological awareness. They should play a large role in any kindergarten curriculum.

Use Rhyming Books

While on the subject of things that have stood the test of time, you may remember being read *Hop on Pop; One Fish, Two Fish, Red Fish, Blue Fish;* and *There's a Wocket in My Pocket*. Books such as these still appeal to the rhythm-, rhyme-, and fun-oriented child who is our kindergartner, and from these books children develop important understandings. You can nudge those understandings on a bit, if you help the children notice that many of the words that rhyme are also spelled alike. As you reread one of these favorite books, let the children point out the rhyming words and make lists of these on the board. Read the words together. Add other words which are spelled like that and rhyme and make rhymes with those. Make up "silly words" and make them rhyme too and decide what they might be and illustrate them! If you can have a wocket in your pocket, you can have a hocket in your pocket. What would a hocket be? What could you do with it?

Do Rhymes and Riddles

Young children are terribly egocentric and they are very "body oriented." In doing rhymes and riddles, therefore, have children point to different body parts to show rhyming words. Tell children that you are going to say some words which rhyme with *head* or *feet*. After you say each word, have the children repeat the word with you and decide if the word rhymes with *head* or *feet.* If the word you say rhymes with *head,* they should point to their head. If it rhymes with *feet,* they should point to their feet. As children point, be sure to respond, acknowledging a correct response by saying something like, "Carl is pointing to his head because *bread* rhymes with *head.*" You may want to use some of these words:

meet	bread
seat	red
bed	beat
dead	greet
led	sleet
sheet	fed
sled	thread
heat	shed

Now, ask the children the following riddles (the answers all rhyme with *head*):

On a sandwich, we put something in between the. . . ?

When something is not living anymore, it is. . . ?

To sew, you need a needle and. . . ?

This is the color of blood. . . ?

We can ride down snowy hills on a. . . ?

Here are other riddles, the answers to which rhyme with *feet:*

Steak and pork chops are different kinds of. . . ?

On a crowded bus, it is hard to get a. . . ?

You make your bed with a. . . ?

When you are cold, you turn on the. . . ?

If children like this activity, do it again, but this time have them listen for words which rhyme with *hand* or *knee.* If the word you say rhymes with *hand,* they should point to their hand. If it rhymes with *knee,* they should point to their knee. Some words to use follow:

sand	band
land	see
me	bee
stand	grand
we	free
brand	tea
tree	and

Here are some riddles for *hand:*

You dig in this at the beach. . . ?

To build a house, you must first buy a piece of. . . ?

The musicians who march and play in a parade are called a. . . ?

You can sit or you can. . . ?

And some more which rhyme with *knee:*

You use your eyes to. . . ?

You could get stung by a. . . ?

If something doesn't cost anything, we say it is. . . ?

You can climb up into a. . . ?

To challenge your stars, have them make up riddles and point for words that rhyme with *feet, knee, hand,* or *head.* As each child gives a riddle, have the riddle giver point to the body part which rhymes with the answer. Model this for the children by doing a few to show them how.

Play Blending and Segmenting Games

Call the children to line up for lunch by saying their names, one sound at a time (P-a-t; R-a-m-o-n-a). As you say each, have the class respond with the name and let that child line up.

As a variation, say a sound and let everyone whose name contains that sound anywhere in it line up. Be sure you have the children respond to the sound and not the letter. If you say "sss," Sam, Jessie and Cynthia can all line up!

Display familiar pictures. Let children take turns saying the names of the pictures—one sound at a time—and calling on another child to identify that picture. In the beginning, limit the pictures to five or six whose names are very different.

Assessing Children's Emerging Literacy

In order to determine how various children are developing in their reading, writing, and word knowledge, teachers need to be keen observers of children. The most practical diagnostic tool I know of for this purpose is Marie

Clay's *An Observation Survey of Early Literacy Achievement*. This survey, first developed as a screening device for Reading Recovery, has been adapted for classroom use. It contains detailed information on how to take and interpret running records which tell you what strategies a child is using while reading and help you determine if the material being read is at the appropriate difficulty level for the reader. In addition to running records, the survey contains procedures for determining how many words children can read and write, their print-tracking ability and their knowledge of letter-sound relationships. This survey is a valid and authentic measure of children's emergent literacy behaviors, and I hope it will become as omnipresent a part of kindergarten and first-grade assessment as the old reading readiness tests used to be!

Many teachers have come up with their own ways of observing children's early reading and writing progress. Here are some critical behaviors to observe as you assess children's development:

1. They read (or pretend read) favorite books and poems/songs/chants.

2. They write in whatever way they can, and they can read what they wrote even if no one else can.

3. They track print—that is, show you what to read and point to the words using left-to-right/top-to-bottom conventions.

4. They know critical jargon, can point to just one word, the first word in the sentence, just one letter, the first letter in the word, the longest word, etc.

5. They recognize and can write some concrete words—their names and names of other children, favorite words from books, poems, and chants.

6. They recognize if words rhyme and can make up rhymes.

7. They can name many letters and tell you words that begin with the common initial sounds.

8. They are learning more about the world they live in and are more able to talk about what they know.

9. They can listen to stories and informational books and retell the most important information

10. They see themselves as readers and writers and new members of the "literacy club."

This chapter has described a variety of activities used by kindergarten and first-grade teachers who want all children to have the foundation needed to become readers and writers. These activities engage the children in reading and writing and help them see how words, letters, and sounds are part of reading and writing. The activities include many different response modes and contain a variety of things to be learned from each so that all children can enjoy and learn from them. Jargon is used only as needed, and the concrete thing represented by the jargon is always there so children learn the words they need to communicate about reading and writing. Finally, the activities are truly activities! The children are active! They are seldom just sitting and listening; they move, sing, chant, act, draw, write, and read.

References

Clay, M. M. (1993). *An Observation Survey of Early Literacy Achievement*. Portsmouth, NH: Heinemann.

Cunningham, P. M., (1988). "Names—A Natural for Early Reading and Writing." *Reading Horizons, 28*, 36–41.

Cunningham, P. M., and Allington, R. L. (1991). "Words, Letters, Sounds and Big Books. *Learning, 20*, 91–95.

Lundberg, I., Frost, J., and Petersen, O-P. (1988). Effects of an Extensive Program for Stimulating Phonological Awareness in Preschool Children." *Reading Research Quarterly, 23*, 264–284.

McCracken, R., and McCracken, M. (1988). *Songs, Stories and Poetry to Teach Reading and Writing*. Manitoba, Canada: Peguis.

Sulzby, E., Teale, W. H., and Kamberelis, G. (1989). "Emergent Writing in the Classroom: Home and School Connections." In D. S. Strickland, and L. M. Morrow (eds.), *Emerging Literacy: Young Children Learn to Read and Write*. Newark, DE: International Reading Association.

Teale, W. H., and Sulzby, E. (1991). "Emergent Literacy." In R. Barr, M. Kamil, P. Mosenthal, and P. D. Pearson (eds.), *Handbook of Reading Research*, Vol. 2. (pp. 418–452). New York: Longman.

2

Little Words

Most of the words we read and write are one-syllable *regular* words, which, because they are consistent with the rules of spelling and pronunciation, we can decode and spell even if we have not seen them before. Developing the ability to independently read and write most regular one-syllable words is a complex process and takes time and practice with a variety of activities. This chapter describes activities successfully used by teachers to help all children become independent at reading and writing one-syllable words.

Making Consonants Useful

Chapter One described a number of activities which help build consonant letter-sound knowledge. If this knowledge is minimal (or nonexistent) in your students, you are not ready for this chapter but should do some of the activities (those relating to key words, names, actions, foods, etc.) suggested in Chapter One. The activities in this chapter assume that children have developed some phonological awareness and know some consonant sounds. This section focuses on activities to help students use consonant knowledge to read and write words. First, however, to review the consonant sounds and as a nifty reminder display, I recommend tongue twisters.

Tongue Twisters

Tongue twisters are wonderful for reviewing consonants, because they give many word examples for the sound and are such fun to say. Do one or two each day. First, just say them and have the students repeat them after you (without letting students see the words). Have students say them as fast as they can and as slowly as they can. When students have said them enough times to have them memorized, have them watch you write them on a chart or poster. Underline the first letter with a different color marker. Have students read them several times. If you are making posters of your tongue twisters, you may want to choose a child to illustrate each.

Add one or two each day—always saying them first and writing only after students have memorized them. After you write the new ones, review all the old ones. Leave the charts or posters displayed, and refer students to them if they forget or become confused about a sound.

Here are some twisters to get you started. You can probably make up better ones. Be sure to use children's names from your class when they have the right letters and sounds!

Cross-Checking Meaning and Consonants

Many words can be figured out by thinking about what would make sense in a sentence and seeing if the consonants in the word match what you are thinking of. The ability to use the consonants in a word along with the context is an important decoding strategy. You must learn to do two things simultaneously—think about what would make sense and think about letters and sounds. Most children would prefer to do one or the other, but not both. Thus, some children guess something that is sensible but ignore the letter sounds they know. Others guess something which is close to the sounds but makes no sense in the sentence! In order to help children cross-check meaning with sound, first have them guess with no letters. There are generally many possibilities for a word that will fit the context. Next, some letters are

Betty's brother, Billy, blew bubbles badly.
Careless Carol couldn't cut cooked carrots.
Dimpled David dawdled during dinner.
Fred's fearless father fell fifty feet.
Gorgeous Gloria got good grades gladly.
Hungry Harry happily had hamburgers.
Jack's jack-o-lantern just jumped Jupiter.
Kevin's kangaroo kicked Karen Kelly.
Lucky Louie liked licking lollipops lazily.
My mama makes many marvelous meatballs.
Naughty Nancy never napped nicely.
Peter Piper picked a peck of pickled peppers.
Rough Roger readily runs relays.
Susie's sister sipped seven sodas swiftly.
Tall Tom took tiny Tim to Texas.
Veronica visited very vicious volcanoes.
Willy went west where Wilbur was waiting.
Yippy yanked young Yolanda's yucky yellow yoyo.
Zany Zelda zapped Zeke's zebra.

revealed and the number of possibilities is narrowed. Finally, show the whole word and help children confirm which guess makes sense and has the right letters.

For each cross-checking lesson, you will need to write sentences on the board or an overhead transparency. Cover the word to be guessed with two pieces of paper, one of which covers only the first letter and when removed will only reveal what the first letter is. (You may want to use magnets to hold the pieces of paper on the board.) Here are some sample sentences. Remember that using your children's names helps to keep them engaged!

Carl likes to go on <u>vacations</u>.
Paula likes to go to the <u>beach</u>.
Miguel likes to go to the <u>mountains</u>.
Sarah likes to go to the <u>zoo</u>.
Vacations are fun for the whole <u>family</u>.

Show the children the sentences, and tell them that they will read each sentence and guess what word you have covered up. Have students read the first sentence and guess what the covered word is. (They may guess *trips, vacations, cruises,* etc.) Next to the sentence, write each guess that makes sense. If a guess does not make sense, explain why, but do not write this guess. A child who guesses *carnivals* for the first sentence should be told, "We go to carnivals and we go on rides at carnivals, but we don't go on carnivals." This explanation will help build their language skills.

When you have written several guesses, remove the paper covering the first letter (*v*). Erase any guesses that do not begin with this letter and ask if there are any more guesses that "makes sense and start with a *v*." If there are more guesses, write these. Be sure all written guesses both make sense and start correctly. Some children will begin guessing anything that begins with *v*. Respond with something like, "*Vine* does begin with a *v*, but I can't write *vine* because people don't like to go on a *vine*"; "Yes, *visits* begins with *v*, and people like to go on visits. I will write *visits*."

When you have written all guesses that make sense and begin correctly, uncover the word. See if the word you uncover is one the children guessed. If the children have the correct guess, praise their efforts. If not, say, "That was a tough one!" and go on to the next sentence. Continue with each sentence going through the same steps:

1. Read the sentence and write any guesses that make sense.

2. Uncover the first letter. Erase any guesses that don't begin with that letter.

3. Have students make more guesses, and write only those that both make sense and begin with the correct letter.

4. Uncover the whole word and see if any one of their guesses was correct.

Word Families plus Consonants

Word families (also called phonograms) consist of words that have the same vowel and ending letters and that rhyme. Once children can make words rhyme and know some consonant letters, you can quickly increase the number of words they can decode by showing them how word families work. There are many different ways to help children learn about word families. Here is a possible beginning lesson. It assumes that children know the words *cat* and *will.* If children do not know these words, choose two other words from which you can make many rhyming words by changing the first consonant. For beginning lessons, choose two words whose sounds are quite different. They should have different initial, vowel, and final sounds.

Take a piece of chart paper and fold it in half, then open it back again. Have children fold and open a piece of small paper just as you have done with the chart paper. Write *cat* at the top of one-half of your chart paper and have children write *cat* on their paper. Write *will* at the top of the other half and have children do the same. Under *cat,* write *hat,* and have children do the same. Read *cat* and *hat,* and have the children read them with you. Then, have the children chant the spelling of *cat* and *hat.* Help children notice that *cat* and *hat* rhyme when you say them and have the same vowel and last letter when you write them. Write *hill* under *will* and have the children write it on their paper. Have *will* and *hill* pronounced and chanted, and make sure children notice that they rhyme and have the same last three letters.

Tell the children that you will say some words that rhyme with *cat* or *will.* They will write the word under *cat* if it rhymes with *cat* and under *will* if it rhymes with *will.* After the children write the words on their paper, ask someone to spell the word and tell you what it rhymes with. Then, write it on the chart in the correct column. If children write a word in the wrong column, have them cross it out and write it in the correct column. If they begin the word with the wrong letter, have them cross that letter out and write the correct letter. Here are some words in the listening vocabularies of most children. Put each word in a sentence after you say it:

| bat | bill | fill | fat | mat | mill |
| pill | pat | rat | sat | Jill | kill |

When all words are written, have the children read with you the rhyming words under *cat* and *will.* Point out words that can also be names (*Bill, Pat*), and write them next to the first one with a capital letter. Let children make some silly sentences using rhyming words, and write a few of these on the board. (*The fat cat is Pat. The pill will kill Jill.*) You may want them to write some silly sentences of their own.

Display the chart on which you wrote these words and add more charts over the next several weeks. As you add charts, have children quickly read the words in the word families already done. There are many word families you can do. Here are some that give you many useful words and that represent the different vowels. To start each chart with these words, be sure to pick one the children know, and to use two that are very different sounding as pairs for the lessons:

Dad	best	bug	red	day	not	sing	old	can	big
bad	nest	dug	bed	bay	cot	ding	bold	Dan	dig
had	pest	hug	fed	Fay	got	ring	cold	fan	fig
mad	rest	jug	led	gay	hot	wing	fold	Jan	jig
pad	test	lug	Ned	hay	Dot	zing	gold	man	pig
sad	vest	mug	Ted	Jay	lot	king	hold	pan	rig
	west	rug	wed	lay	pot		sold	ran	wig
		tug		may	rot		told	tan	
				pay				van	
				Ray					
				say					

As you do these lessons and add charts of rhyming words, help children realize that words with the same vowel and ending letters usually rhyme. When they come to a word in their reading that they don't know, they might be able to figure it out by thinking of a word they know that has the same vowel and ending letters.

Making Digraphs Useful

Once children are beginning to use what they know about consonants to read and write words, they should learn some special letter combinations. To teach the digraphs, *sh, ch, th,* and *wh,* it is important that children know some key words that begin with these. If you used actions to teach the initial sounds (as suggested in Chapter One), you may want to add actions for the digraphs:

cheer

shiver

think

whistle

If children have enjoyed the consonant tongue twisters, you may want to add some for the digraphs:

Chief Charlie cheerfully chomped chili cheeseburgers.

Whitney whispered while Wheeler White whistled.

Shy Sheila shot Sharon's shaggy sheep.

Thirty-three thieves thundered through thick thorns.

For both the actions and tongue twisters, make sure that you underline the first two letters *sh, ch, th,* and *wh.* Help children to realize that these two letters have a special sound that is very different from the sound they have when they are by themselves. Then engage children in the two activities described for consonants: Cross-Checking and Word Families.

Cross-Checking Meaning with Digraphs

Do lessons as for consonants, except include words with *s, sh, c, ch, t, th, w,* and *wh.* When the beginning sound is *sh, ch, th,* or *wh,* have your first piece of paper cover both these letters. Some words to get you started:

Carol is <u>sad</u>.
Roberta is <u>shy</u>.
Bob likes to eat <u>corn</u>.
Susanna likes to eat <u>chocolate</u>.
Carol woke up and heard loud <u>talking</u>.
Wendy woke up and heard loud <u>thunder</u>.
Willy went to the zoo to see the <u>whale</u>.
Jack went to the zoo to see the <u>walrus</u>.

Word Families plus Digraphs

If you have made charts for some word families, add *ch, sh, th,* and *wh* words to them. To the ones listed previously, you could add *chat, chill, Chad, chest, shed, shot, that, thug, thing, than.* You may want to add some new word families. Follow the every-pupil response procedure described for consonants, in which children write rhyming words on their papers as you write them on the charts. Here are some word families which include several *ch, sh, th, wh* words and some useful single-consonant words:

in	back	lip	meat	hop	my
fin	Jack	dip	beat	cop	by
pin	Mack	hip	heat	mop	shy
sin	pack	nip	neat	pop	why
tin	rack	rip	seat	top	
win	sack	sip	cheat	chop	
chin	tack	tip	wheat	shop	
thin	shack	chip			
	whack	ship			
		whip			

Making Blends Useful

At first glance, teaching the blends would appear to be an easy task. In fact, some people wonder why we have to teach them at all since they are the same sounds students already know, just blended together. The experience of many teachers and the research of linguists, however, indicate that the blends are quite difficult for many children (Treiman, 1988). Preschool children's speech is commonly marked by blend confusions: "I dwopped it" instead of *I dropped it.* "Top it" instead of *Stop it.*

If your children just infer the sounds of blends once they know the single consonant sounds, skip this section! If they have difficulty, here are some activities we have had good success with.

Teaching the Blends

The first blends are the most difficult to teach, because children must learn to listen for very fine sound differentiations. Deciding which blends to teach first is an arbitrary decision, but I would avoid the *s* blends simply because there are so many of them! This lesson sequence will teach students to distinguish *dr* from *d,* then *tr* from *t,* finally *dr* from *tr.* Before teaching any blends, it is critical that your children know at least one (although, two is better) word that begins with that blend. Known words will function as key words in helping them remember the letter-sound associations.

Draw lines to divide your board into three columns; head one with *d,* one with *r,* and one with *dr.* Write one or two known words that begin with *d, r,* and *dr* to head each column. Give each child a *d* and an *r* letter card, or have each child write *d* on one piece of scrap paper and *r* on another. Children should write these letters big and bold so that you can see them when they display them.

Have children read the known words which head the columns on the board (*down, dog; run, right; draw, dragon*). Say words which begin with *d, r,* or *dr.* Have children hold up the *d,* the *r,* or both the *d* and *r* to show you what column to write the word in. Acknowledge someone with the correct response, and ask that child to tell you what letters you should begin writing the word with. If children give the wrong response, tell them what word it would be with, or without, the *r.* (Do you know what *drive* would be without the *r?* It would be *dive.* Do you drive a car or dive a car? *Drive* needs *d* and *r* blended together to make it *drive.*) Some words you might use are:

drive	duck	raw	dip
drink	drop	drag	dig
dish	dentist	rocket	dark
drew	rocks	drill	rain

Do a similar lesson for *tr,* heading three columns with known words (*ten, tall; run, right; train, tree*) and then having children respond by showing the appropriate letters. If children give the wrong response, tell them what word it would be with, or without, the *r.* (Do you know what *track* would be without the *r?* It would be a *tack.* Does a train go on a track or a tack? *Track* needs *t* and *r* blended together to make it *track.*)

track	trunk	rash	time
trip	true	tip	tail
trail	ten	trap	trick
ring	rip	trash	traffic

Next, do a lesson in which you call out words with *d, r, t, tr,* and *dr.* Head five columns with the known words and give all students the letters *d, r,* and *t.* Try to call out some words where the beginning sound is what differentiates them. Here are some possible words:

Rick	dry	rip	troop
tick	try	tip	droop
trick		trip	
Dick		drip	
		dip	

Once children understand how sounds are blended together and how leaving out a letter or adding a letter often changes the word, you can teach the other blends more quickly. You may want to do a lesson on *b, bl, br;* one on *c, cl, cr;* one on *f, fl, fr;* and, then, one on the most common *s* blends. Do these lessons in the same way, by heading columns with known words and letting children hold up letters to show you where to write the words. Acknowledge correct responses and let children know what word it would be with or without the needed letter.

ANOTHER APPROACH TO BLENDS

For some children, it is easier to blend a letter on to a word they already know. To show children this alternative way of looking at words that begin with blends, write some words on the board which can be changed by adding a single letter. Make five columns on the board, and have the students make five columns on a sheet of paper. Head these columns with the words *ran, ray, Rick, rip,* and *ride,* and have students write these words on their paper.

Under *ran,* write *ran* two more times. Have students do the same on their papers. Then tell them that they can make two new words by adding a letter to the beginning of *ran.* Have students add *b* and have the word *bran* identified. Then, add *F* and have the name *Fran* identified.

Continue to the next column, and write *ray* three times, then add letters to write *gray, pray,* and *tray.* Finish the other columns with *brick, trick; trip, grip, drip;* and *bride, pride.* Help students to verbalize that if they see a word beginning with another letter and then an *r,* they can often figure out how to read the word by thinking what it would be with just the *r* and then adding the sound of the first letter to that.

Another lesson can be done by having students head columns with the words *lump, lot, lay, lack,* and *lick,* and having students write the words again, and then having them add letters to write *clump, plump,* and *slump; blot, clot, plot,* and *slot; clay* and *play; black, clack,* and *slack; click* and *slick.*

Adding a final letter to known words to change them into other words is also an effective way of showing students how final blends work. Students can write *an, men, Ben, car,* and *Stan* and, then, add a *d* to magically change them to *and, mend, bend, card,* and *stand.* They can write *bar, bun, sun, pin,* and *thin* and, just by adding a *k,* have *bark, bunk, sunk, pink,* and *think.* By adding a *t* to *Ben, den, ten, tin, pan, ran, star, bun,* and *run,* they will have *bent, dent, tent, tint, pant, rant, start, bunt,* and *runt.* These kinds of word-manipulation activities are very important for children, because as they add or take away letters and create new words they can read and write, they gain some control over this mysterious code that is English spelling.

Tongue Twisters with Blends

The following are some blend tongue twisters children enjoy saying and illustrating:

Blind Blanche's blueberries bloomed and blossomed.

Brenda's brother Brad brought Brenda bread for breakfast.

Claire's class clapped for the clumsy clown.

Craig crocodile crawled 'cross crooked crawling creepies.

Drew dreamed dreadful dragons dropped Drew's drum.

Flip's flat flounder flops and floats.

Freddie's friend Fran fries frogs.

Gloria's glittery glasses glow.

Grouchy Grace grows green grapes.

Sleepy Slick slipped on a slimy, slippery sled.

Smarty Smurf smashed smelly, smoky smokebombs.

Sneaky Snoopy snatched snowman's snazzy sneakers.

Sparky's special spaceship speeded into spectacular space.

A stegosaurus stepped on Steven's stepsister, Stephanie.

Swifty Swan's sweetheart swims, swirls, sways, and swoops.

Scary skeleton skipped over skinny Scout's skunk.

Tracy transformed triple transformers into trains and trucks.

Actions with Blends

If children learned consonant and digraph actions, you may want them to learn some blend actions:

blink	grab	stand still
breathe	plant	track
cry	swim	twist
climb	skate	
drive	sleep	
fly	smile	
frown	spin	

Cross-Checking Meaning with Blends

Do lessons in which some of the targeted words begin with the single letter and some begin with a blend. Cover the word with two pieces of paper, the first covering the single letter or the blend. Pair the sentences to make the contrast clear. Here are a few to get you started:

Carl has a big <u>brother</u>.
David has a big <u>bike</u>.
Julio has a big <u>bloodhound</u>.
Maggie lost her <u>slippers</u>.
Carolyn lost her <u>sneakers</u>.
Justin lost his pet <u>spider</u>.
Carlos lost his <u>sweatshirt</u>.
Paul lost his <u>sandwich</u>.

Word Families plus Blends

If you have charts for word families, add words to those that begin with blends as children learn the blends. You may want to add some new word families. Here are some which give you many useful single consonant and digraph words and lots of blend words. These, added to the ones listed earlier for consonants and digraphs, give you 28 of the most useful word families and give students access to hundreds of words they can read and write.

rain	bank	cash	deep	fight
gain	Hank	dash	jeep	light
main	rank	gash	keep	might
pain	sank	hash	peep	night
vain	tank	lash	seep	right
chain	yank	mash	weep	sight
brain	thank	rash	sheep	tight
drain	blank	sash	creep	bright
grain	clank	clash	sleep	flight
plain	crank	crash	steep	fright
Spain	drank	flash	sweep	slight
stain	Frank	slash		
train	plank	smash		
sprain	prank	stash		
strain	spank	trash		
	stank			
Dick	pink	coke	dock	bunk
kick	link	joke	lock	dunk
lick	mink	poke	rock	hunk
Nick	rink	woke	sock	junk
pick	sink	choke	tock	punk
Rick	wink	broke	shock	sunk
sick	think	smoke	block	chunk
tick	blink	spoke	clock	drunk
chick	clink	stroke	flock	flunk
thick	drink		smock	skunk
brick	stink		stock	spunk
click	shrink			stunk
flick				trunk
slick				shrunk
stick				
trick				

Endings

Before going on to the complex task of helping children understand how our vowel system works, we should consider what students need to be taught about endings. The most common endings are, of course, the *s* that makes nouns plural and the *-s, -ed,* and *-ing* endings on verbs. Many children figure these out on their own because of their oral language knowledge. Some children become confused, however, when they see a known word with an ending, particularly when some kind of spelling change is involved.

The principles for teaching endings are the same as for teaching any other strategies. Make sure children have something known to which they can relate the abstract principles you are teaching. Keep the jargon and rules to a minimum. Display key sentences and pictures as a reminder. You might choose a big book, or a class book, or a language experience chart which the children are very familiar with and use it to point to words with these endings.

If you have been using and displaying tongue twisters in your room, you already have the known words and the display ready and need only to draw student's conscious attention to the endings in them. Have them reread a few that have the *s* plural. For example:

Hungry Harry happily had hamburgers.

Smarty Smurf smashed smelly, smoky smokebombs.

Tracy transformed triple transformers into trains and trucks.

After reading these a few times, have students watch while you underline the ending s̲ in *hamburgers, smokebombs, transformers, trains,* and *trucks.* Help them to see that the *-s* means there are more than one. Then write on the board some words students know:

girl   boy   house   school   teacher

Have children add an *s* to these words, and talk about how you can change words when you are writing to show they mean more than one.

Leave the three tongue twisters with the underlined *s,* showing plural, displayed and remind students as they come to plural words in their reading and need them in their writing. At this early stage, I would not focus on spelling changes such as changing *y* to *i,* but I would simply point those out as the opportunities present themselves.

In selecting these three tongue twisters, I purposely excluded those that had other *-s* endings in addition to the *-s* plural ending. Once children are comfortable with the -*s* plural ending, you may want to teach the -*s, -ed,* and -*ing* verb endings. Again, use some known sentences from big books, class books, or experience charts, or use the tongue twisters. Begin by rereading the familiar text and identifying -*s* plural endings. Then, underline the endings you want to teach, and draw children's attention to the ending by showing them that we "just naturally add these to the words when we say them, and these are the letters we use to write them." If you have tongue twisters displayed, you might use:

Grouchy Grace grow_s_ green grapes.

My mama make_s_ many marvelous meatballs.

Peter Piper pick_ed_ a peck of pickled peppers.

Veronica visit_ed_ very vicious volcanoes.

Lucky Louie lik_ed_ lick_ing_ lollipops lazily.

Willy went west where Wilbur was wait_ing_.

Although -*s* plural and -*s, -ed,* and -*ing* are the most useful endings to teach, the tongue twisters contain wonderful examples for -*'s* and -*ly.* If you are using the tongue twisters to provide the known examples, you might just as well go ahead and take the opportunity to teach these two endings also. You might use:

Betty_'s_ brother Billy blew bubbles bad_ly_.

Gorgeous Gloria got good grades glad_ly_.

Jack_'s_ jack-o-lantern just jumped Jupiter.

Kevin_'s_ kangaroo kicked Karen Kelly.

Naughty Nancy never napped nice_ly_.

Susie_'s_ sister sipped seven sodas swift_ly_.

Yippy yanked young Yolanda_'s_ yucky yellow yoyo.

Blind Blanche_'s_ blueberries bloomed and blossomed.

Freddie_'s_ friend Fran fries frogs.

Some children do need practice to become automatic at adding endings to words as they write, particularly when the words require spelling changes. In the next chapter, you will find some quick activities for providing practice with endings as you review the spelling of high-frequency words on the word wall.

Vowel Strategies—Decoding and Spelling by Analogy

In English, the vowels are the most variant and unpredictable. The letter *a* commonly represents the sound in *and, made, agree, art, talk,* and *care.* We have given names to some of these sounds. *And* has a short *a; made* has a long *a; agree* is a schwa; the *a* in *art* is *r* controlled. We don't even have names for the sound *a* represents in *talk* and *care.* Further complicating things are the many words in which *a* doesn't do any of these six common things—*eat, coat, legal*—and the fact that even the consistent sounds can be spelled in many different ways. The long *a* sound is commonly spelled by the patterns in *made, maid,* and *may.* The sound *a* has in *talk* is spelled by an *aw* in *saw* and an *au* in *Paul.*

When you stop to think about all the possible sounds and spelling patterns for the vowels, you marvel at the fact that anyone becomes an accurate and fast decoder of English words. And yet, that is exactly what happens! All good readers could quickly and accurately pronounce the made-up words *gand, hade, afuse, sart, malk, lare, jeat, foat, pregal, maw,* and *naul.* Just don't ask them to explain how they did it!

In schools we have traditionally taught students many rules and jargon: the *e* on the end makes the vowel long; vowels in unaccented syllables have a schwa sound; when a vowel is followed by *r,* it is *r* controlled. We have taught so many rules and jargon because it takes over 200 rules to account for the common spelling patterns in English. Although these rules do describe our English alphabetic system, it is doubtful that readers and writers use these rules to decode and spell words. So, how do they do it?

Research (Adams, 1990) supports the view that readers decode words by using spelling patterns from the words they know. *Made, fade, blade,* and *shade* all have the same spelling pattern, and the *a* is pronounced the same in all four. When you see the made-up word, *hade,* your mind accesses that known spelling pattern and you give the made-up word the same pronunciation you have for other words with that spelling pattern. Spelling patterns are letters that are commonly seen together in a certain position in words. The *al* at the end of *legal, royal,* and the made-up word *pregal* is a spelling pattern. Sometimes a spelling pattern can be a single letter, as the *a* is in *agree, about, adopt,* and the made-up word *afuse.* Using words you know to decode unknown words is called decoding by analogy.

Spelling patterns are quite reliable indicators of pronunciation—with two exceptions. The first exception is that the most frequently used words are often not pronounced like other words with that spelling pattern. *To* and *do* should rhyme with *go, so,* and *no. Have* should rhyme with *gave, save,* and *brave. Said* should rhyme with *maid* and *paid.* Linguists deal with this contradiction by explaining that the way words are pronounced changes across centuries of use. The words used most frequently are the ones whose pronunciation has changed the fastest! This explanation, although true, is little consolation to teachers who must teach the most common words to children beginning to read, and at the same time must teach them to look for patterns and predictability! Because the most common words cannot be decoded or correctly spelled by relying on sound and spelling patterns, and because children need to read and write these common words in order to read and write anything, children need much and early practice with these common words. (Activities for teaching words you can't decode and shouldn't invent-spell are the focus of Chapter Three.)

The second exception in spelling patterns is that some spelling patterns have two common sounds. The *ow* at the end of words occurs in *show, grow,* and *slow,* but also in *how, now,* and *cow.* The *ood* at the end of *good, hood,* and *stood* is also found at the end of *food, mood,* and *brood.* Children who are constantly cross-checking meaning with the pronunciations they come up with will not be bothered by these differences, as long as the word they are reading is in their listening-meaning vocabulary.

Whereas spelling patterns work wonderfully well for pronouncing unfamiliar words, they don't work as well for spelling! There are often two or more spelling patterns with the same pronunciation. When trying to read the made-up word *nade,* you would simply compare its pronunciation to other words with that spelling pattern—*made, grade, blade.* If, however, I didn't show you *nade,* but rather pronounced it and asked you to spell it, you might compare it to *maid, paid,* and *braid* and spell it n-a-i-d. Most words can be correctly pronounced by comparing them to known spelling patterns. To spell a word correctly, however, you must often choose between two or more possible spelling patterns.

So, what should we do about helping children learn to read and write words with the correct sounds and spelling patterns? Much of what we should do has already been discussed in this chapter. Cross-checking helps children use both letter-sound and meaning information. They can quickly disambiguate spelling patterns with two or more pronunciations by making sure what they say makes sense to them. Word families are, in effect, spelling patterns. Children who learn many common word families also learn something more important—to look carefully at the spelling pattern of a new word and search through the words they already know for words with the same spelling pattern.

There are, however, some specific activities we can do with children to move them toward independent decoding and spelling. In the remainder of this chapter, activities are described that teach the analogy decoding and spelling strategy. These activities assume that children have a good understanding of how to use consonants, digraphs, and blends to read and write words, are in the habit of cross-checking meaning with letter-sound relationships, and know many word families.

Word Sorts

Word Sorts (Henderson, 1990) are a wonderfully versatile activity for helping children develop the habit of analyzing words to look for patterns. There are a variety of ways to do word sorts, but the basic principles are the same. Children look at words and sort them into categories based on spelling patterns and sound. Children say the words and look at how they are spelled. They learn that to go in a certain category, the words must "sound the same and look the same." Sorting can be done with pictures, with initial sounds, with rhyming words, with vowel patterns, and with sophisticated multisyllabic patterns. (Many word-sort examples can be found in a wonderful new book, *Words Their Way* by Donald Bear, Marcia Invernizzi, and Shane Templeton.)

Once children can sort pictures and can sort for initial sounds, they are ready to sort for rhymes. I like to begin with three or four words that are very different in look and sound so that children experience success and understand what they are doing. For the first several sorts, I make sure that the words have different vowels and different ending letters. An early sort might include the three words *big*, *ran*, and *old* as category headers. The children would then be shown rhyming words and would put them in the correct place. Later, rhyming word sorts would include only words with the same vowel. The words *ran*, *at*, and *back*, for example.

As children become sophisticated at sorting rhyming words, sorting usually shifts to including all words with a particular vowel sound and is not restricted to rhyming words. The children are generally given three cate-

[handwritten margin notes: 1. pictures 2. beg. sounds 3. rhymes 4. vowels]

gories and an "other" category for words that don't fit—either because they don't look the same or don't sound the same. A word sort might have these categories:

hat	make	rain	?

The words to be sorted might include:

back	stamp	shade
paid	said	what
ham	champ	cave
have	face	stab
law	crab	pail
crash	sail	jam

This sorting by vowels is much more sophisticated than rhyming words, and requires the children to think about the sound of each vowel separately from the rest of the word. Notice also the words that would go under the ? category. *Have* looks like the other *a-e* words but does not sound the same. *What* looks like the other *a* words and *said* looks like the other *ai* words but the sounds are different.

The sorting itself can occur in a variety of whole-class, small-group, and partner formats. Sometimes, teachers use the big chalkboard divided into columns to write the words as children write them on individual chalk-boards. Another popular format is to have the words written in boxes on a photocopied sheet. The children cut them apart and working with a partner or a small group put them in the appropriate place on a sorting board. Many teachers include word-sorting games such as Word Concentration, Go Fish for Words, and Word Rummy.

There is also variation in the amount of teacher input given to the sort. In a closed sort, the teacher gives the children the category headings. In an open sort, the children work with the words and determine what the categories should be. Most teachers begin with closed-sort activities and as children begin to realize how words can be categorized move to more open sorts.

It is important that children develop speed and automaticity as they sort. Many teachers begin by showing the children the words and then have the children say the words and put them in the appropriate category. When the children are good at looking, saying, and deciding, the teacher leads them in

After reading and enjoying *In a People House* (Le Sieg, 1972), the children rounded up the words that contained the letter O. The teacher wrote them on index cards and placed them in the pocket chart. The children will sort them into different groups, based on their various letter-sound and semantic features. The second photo shows how the children rounded up the rhymes from all these O words.

some "blind" sorting. The teacher or group leader calls out same words already sorted but does not show them to the children (thus *blind* sort). Children decide in which column the word should be written before the word is shown. The children indicate where they think the word should go and then the teacher or group leader shows them the word to confirm, and the word is written in the correct column. The final stage in developing automaticity is spelling certain patterns in the *blind writing* sort. After working with certain words in look, say, and decide sorts and in blind sorts, the teacher or group leader calls out the previously sorted words, and children write them in the appropriate column before seeing them. Once the children have written the word, the teacher or group leader shows the word so that they may confirm their spelling and categorization.

In most classrooms, word sorts are followed by word hunts. Many teachers post charts with the categories the class has worked on, and children are encouraged to add words that fit the pattern any time they find them in anything they are reading. Some children keep word notebooks and add words they find that fit particular categories. Hunting for words is a critical transfer step because it draws children's attention to spelling patterns in the real materials they are reading.

Making Words

Making Words (Cunningham and Cunningham, 1992; Cunningham and Hall, 1994) is an activity in which children are given some letters and use these letters to make words. They make little words and then bigger words until the final word is made. The final word always includes all the letters they have, and children are always eager to figure out what the word is that can be made from all the letters. Making words is an active, hands-on, manipulative activity in which children learn how to look for patterns in words and how changing just one letter or where you put a letter changes the whole word. Here is an example of a Making Words Lesson done in one classroom.

For this lesson, each child had six consonants (*c, d, f, f, l, r*) and two vowels (*i* and *o*). In the pocket chart at the front of the room, the teacher had large cards with the same letters. Her cards, like the small letter cards used by the children, had the uppercase letter on one side and lowercase letter on the other side. The consonant letters were written in black and the two vowels were in red.

The teacher began by making sure that each child had all the letters needed. "What two vowels will we use to make words today?" she asked. The children held up their red *i* and *o* and responded appropriately.

The children have made the words *if*, *of*, and *off*. After they make these words, index cards on which they are written are placed in the pocket chart.

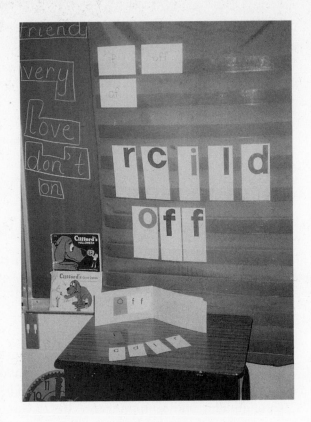

The teacher then wrote the numeral *2* on the board and said, "We will make some easy two-letter words first to get warmed up. Take two letters and make *if*. I wonder if it will snow this weekend. Everyone say *if*. The children all said the word *if* and quickly put the *i* and the *f* in their holders to spell this word most of them knew. As the children made *if*, the teacher circulated and tapped a child who had the word *if* made correctly to go and make *if* with the pocket chart letters. She then put an index card with the word *if* in the pocket chart.

"We are going to make one more two-letter word today. The word I am thinking of is *of*. Everyone say *of*. Change your vowel and you can change *if* to *of*." The children quickly spelled *of* in their holders and one child was tapped to go and spell *of* with the pocket chart letters. The teacher put the index card with the word *of* in the pocket chart.

Next, she erased the *2* and wrote a *3* on the board. "Add a letter to *of* and you will have the word *off*. Turn the TV off. Everyone say *off*." The lesson continued with children making words with their individual letter cards, a child going to the pocket chart to make the word, and the teacher putting a card with that word in the pocket chart.

The children made two more three-letter words, *oil* and *old*. The teacher erased the *3* and wrote a *4* on the board and asked them to add just one letter to *old* to make the word *fold*. Next they changed one letter to change *fold* to *cold*. At this point, the teacher said, "Don't take any letters out and don't add any. Just change where the letters are and you can change *cold* into *clod*."

They then made *cord*, *lord*, *Ford*, *foil*, and *coil*. When the teacher asked them to make the word *Ford*, she used this sentence,

My son David drives a white Ford Taurus.

She then circulated around looking to see who had the word *Ford* spelled correctly so that she could choose someone to make it with the pocket chart letters.

"Oh, dear," she moaned. "No one has the word *Ford* spelled correctly. I guess I'll get to make it with the pocket chart letters this time." The children looked at her in amazement and then quickly looked at their letters *f-o-r-d* to see what the problem might be. Suddenly, one child caught on and turned her *f* over to the capital *F* side. This child was sent to the pocket chart and the other children quickly realized that *Ford* was a name—a name of a particular car. They knew that names needed capital letters but had never before realized that car names needed them too!

The teacher erased the *4* and wrote a *5* and they used five of their letters to make the word *cliff*.

Then the teacher said, "There are no more big words I could think of, except, of course, for the word that can be made with all the letters. I will be looking to see who has figured out the word we can make with all these letters and can make that word."

The children were all busy manipulating their letters trying to come up with the word. They knew that each lesson ended with a word that used all their letters, and they always liked to figure it out. On some days, most children had the big word figured out and were ready to spell it when the teacher indicated it was time to, but today everyone was stumped. The teacher let them move their letters around for a minute and then began giving them some clues.

"It's a name. . . . It begins with your letter *C*. . . ."

The children all quickly put their capital *C* in their holders and continued moving the letters around trying to make them into a word. All of a sudden, several children caught on at once. "It's Clifford!" they shouted in amazement. Quickly and gleefully, everyone made the name of the very popular big red dog. As a child went to the pocket chart to arrange all the letters to spell *Clifford*, another child noticed the Clifford books sitting not too far away. "They were here all the time," he bemoaned, "and I didn't figure it out!"

After all the children had *Clifford* made in their holders, the teacher had them close their holders, and together they read all the words they had made which were lined up in the pocket chart:

if of off oil old fold cold clod cord lord Ford foil oil cliff Clifford

The children knew that after making all the words, they sorted these words into patterns and then talked about how these words would help you spell other words. The teacher picked up *old*, placed it at the bottom of the pocket chart and asked,

"Who can come and hand me two words that rhyme with *old*?"

A child handed her the words *fold* and *cold*, which she placed under the word *old*. Together they spelled and pronounced the three rhyming words *o-l-d*; *c-o-l-d*; *f-o-l-d*. Reminding the children that thinking of a rhyming word was a good strategy for figuring out how to pronounce new words, the teacher wrote the words *gold* and *scold* on the board and the children decoded *gold* and *scold* using the *o-l-d* pattern. She then reminded them that thinking of rhyming words could also help them when they were writing and needed to spell a word.

Next time the teacher asked, "What if you were writing and you wanted to write, *My Mom told me to come right home*, *but I forgot*, how would you spell *told*?"

The children easily spelled *told* using *old*, *fold*, and *cold* as models. They continued sorting out the rhyming word. The used *oil*, *coil*, and *foil* to read the words *boil* and *broil* and to spell *spoil*. They sorted out *cord*, *lord*, and *Ford*, and the teacher told them she thought that was all the words they might read and write with the *o-r-d* pattern. Several children noticed that the last part of Clifford ended in *o-r-d* and almost rhymed with

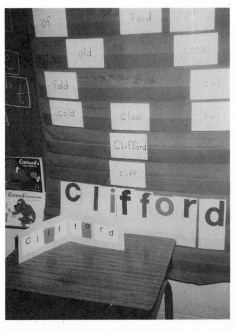

In the first photo, the children have sorted out the rhymes. The next photo shows how they sorted out the words beginning with *cl*.

cord, *lord*, and *Ford*. They also sorted the words that begin with *cl*—*clod*, *cliff*, and *Clifford*—and the two names that began with capital letters—*Ford* and *Clifford*.

As you can see from this sample lesson, Making Words is an activity which keeps the children involved and helps them learn to look for patterns. To plan a Making-Words lesson, you begin with the word you want to end with. Many teachers choose this word from a book or story that children have been reading. You write this word on an index card and then consider what other words you could have the children make. There are always more words than you can make in a fifteen-minute lesson, so you select the words and the order in which you have the children make them so that they begin to see that when you change or add a letter, the word changes in a predictable way.

Here are three Making-Words lessons based on children's books. The words are stored in these envelopes on which the words to be made are written on the right and patterns to sort for are written on the left. Some teachers store these envelopes of Making Words lessons in a big box in the teacher workroom so that all teachers can share the lessons.

Steps in Planning a Making-Words Lesson

1. Decide what the "big word" is that can be made with all the letters. In choosing this word, consider books the children are reading, and what letter-sound patterns you can draw children's attention to through the sorting at the end.

2. Make a list of other words you can make from these letters.

3. From all the words you could make, pick 12 to 15 words using these criteria:

    a. Words that you can sort for the pattern you want to emphasize.

    b. Little words and big words so that the lesson is a multilevel lesson. (Making the little words helps your slowest students; making the big words challenges your most accelerated students.)

    c. Words that can be made with the same letters in different places (cold/clod) so that children are reminded that when spelling words, the ordering of the letters is crucial.

    d. A proper name or two to remind them that names—even automobile names!—need capital letters.

    e. Words that most students have in their listening vocabularies.

4. Write all the words on index cards and order them from smallest to biggest.

5. Once you have the two-letter, three-letter, etc. words together, order them so that you can emphasize letter patterns and how changing the position of the letters or changing/adding just one letter results in a different word.

6. Store the cards in an envelope. Write on the envelope the words in order and the patterns you will sort for.

Steps in Teaching a Making-Words Lesson

1. Place the large letter cards needed in a pocket chart or along the chalk ledge.

2. Have designated children give a holder and one letter to each child. Let the passer keep the Ziploc bag or paper cup containing that letter and have the same child collect that letter when the lesson is over.

3. Hold up and name the letters on the large letter cards and have the children hold up their matching small letter cards.

4. Write the numeral *2* (or *3* if there are no two-letter words in this lesson) on the board and have the children hold up two fingers. Tell them to take two letters and make the first word. Put the word in a sentence after you say the word.

5. Have a child who has the first word made correctly make the same word with the large letter cards on the chalk ledge or pocket chart. Encourage anyone who didn't make the word correctly at first to fix the word when they see it made correctly.

6. Continue to make the remaining two-letter words, giving students clues such as "Change just the first letter" or "Move the same letters around and you can make a different word" or "Take all your letters out and make another word." Send children who have the word made correctly to make that word with the large letter cards.

7. Erase the *2* and write a *3* on the board. Have the children hold up three fingers and tell them that these words will take three of their letters.

8. Continue having them make words, erasing and changing the number on the board to indicate the number of letters needed. Use the words in simple sentences to make sure they access meaning. Remember to cue them about whether they are just changing one letter, changing letters around, or taking all their letters out to make a word from scratch. When you have them make a name, cue them that it is a name and send a child who has started that name with a capital letter to make the word with the big letters.

9. Before telling them the last word, ask, "Has anyone figured out what word we can make with all our letters?" If so, congratulate them and have them make it. If not, say something like, "I love it when I can stump you." Give them clues to help them figure out the big word.

10. Once all the words have been made, have them close their holders and direct their attention to the words in the pocket chart. Have the children say and spell the words with you as you do this. Use these words for sorting and pointing out patterns. Pick a word and point out a particular spelling pattern, and ask children to find the others with that same pattern. Line these words up so that the pattern is visible.

11. To get maximum transfer to reading and writing, have them use the patterns they have sorted to read and spell a few new words. Emphasize that good readers and writers need to read and spell many words and that thinking of rhyming and other patterns will help you read and spell lots of words.

Using Words You Know

There are hundreds of spelling patterns commonly found in one-syllable words. Word-family instruction helps children understand that words with the same vowel and ending letters usually rhyme and shows them how many words they can read and write by thinking about the initial sound and the word family. This is all critical preparation for what you actually must do when you see a word you haven't seen before. Imagine that a young reader encounters the word *blob*. In order to use spelling patterns to decode that word, she must (1) realize this is an unknown word and look carefully at each letter; (2) ask herself something like, "Do I know any other words spelled like that?"; (3) search through the store of known words in her head looking for ones spelled with an *o-b* at the end; (4) find some words, perhaps *Bob* and *job*; (5) pronounce *blob* like *Bob* and *job*; (6) reread the sentence to cross-check pronunciation and meaning.

As shown above, this is a fairly complex mental strategy, and some children who have all the prerequisites in place—words they can spell with the same spelling pattern, an understanding that words with the same spelling pattern usually rhyme, and the automatic habit of cross-checking—don't know how to orchestrate all this. The following series of lessons is designed to help children "put it all together."

LESSON ONE

Pick three words your students know that have many rhyming words they aren't apt to know. (Since they know the words in the word families you have been using, you probably want to pick other words to use for these lessons. For the first several lessons, pick words whose spelling pattern is quite different.) For this lesson, I have chosen *job*, *nine*, and *map*. Using an overhead projector or drawing paper, write a sentence in which you use a word that rhymes with *job*, *nine*, or *map*. Cover all (by placing paper over it on the overhead projector or by folding the drawing paper) but the word you want students to decode.

Place a sheet of chart paper on your board, divide it into three columns, and head each with *job*, *nine*, or *map*. Have your students do the same on a sheet of paper. Tell students that you will show them a word that rhymes with either *job*, *nine*, or *map*. When you show them the word, have them write it in the column under the rhyming word, then have them use the rhyming word to decode the new word. Have them verbalize the strategy they are using by saying something like, "If n-i-n-e is nine, s-p-i-n-e must be spine." Record the words in the correct column of your chart once students tell you where to put it. Finally, reveal the sentence and have students explain how the word they decoded makes sense in the sentence. Save the chart you made to use in the next lesson. Do five or six sentences in each lesson. For example:

> **The old man injured his *spine*.**
> **The city was destroyed by a big blue *blob*.**
> **The man ran from the angry *mob*.**
> **When we like a show, we *clap*.**
> **The tallest tree is a *pine*.**
> **The math test was a *snap*.**

Conclude the lesson by having students read the known words—*job*, *nine*, and *map*—and the rhyming words—*blob*, *mob*; *spine*, *pine*; *clap*, *snap*. Help them to verbalize the procedure that when you come to a word you don't recognize, you should look at all the letters in it and then see if you know any other words with similar spelling that might rhyme.

LESSON TWO

Tape the chart from lesson one back on the board and review the known and rhyming words. Tape another chart next to it and write one more known word—*tell*—on this chart. Have students divide a sheet of paper into four columns and head each with the known words, *job*, *nine*, *map*, and *tell*. Do five or six sentences with words that rhyme with all four known words. Follow the procedure from lesson one of having students write the new word under the rhyming word, and use the rhyming word to pronounce the new word. (If t-e-l-l is *tell*, s-h-e-l-l must be *shell*.) Then, reveal the sentence and have students explain how the meaning lets them cross-check the pronunciation they came up with. Following are some sentences and words you might use:

The turtle hides in his *shell*.

The old shoes had a very bad *smell*.

Cucumbers grow on a *vine*.

The animal was caught in a *trap*.

I have an old bike I'd like to *sell*.

We eat corn on the *cob*.

Conclude the lesson by having all the rhyming words read, and help children verbalize how they can use words they know to figure out those they don't know; then, have them reread the sentence to check themselves. Save the chart for lessons three and four.

LESSON THREE

Add a fifth known word to the chart—perhaps, *jump*. Have students label columns with all five words and show sentences containing words that rhyme with the five known words—for example, *stump*, *grump*, *dine*, *strap*, *swell*, *dump*.

LESSON FOUR

Add a sixth known word—perhaps *make*. Have students label columns with all six words and show sentences which contain words that rhyme—perhaps *flake*, *shake*, *rob*, *plump*, *line*, *bell*.

LESSONS FIVE TO EIGHT

Do the whole procedure again, starting with three known words for lesson five and building with each additional lesson until students are comparing six new words in lesson eight. You may want to use *made*, *ball*, *need*, *ride*, *frog*, and *but*, and you may have students decode words such as *shut*, *nut*, *cut*, *jog*, *log*, *hog*, *spade*, *fade*, *grade*, *shade*, *trade*, *small*, *stall*, *mall*, *fall*, *wide*, *slide*, *bride*, *hide*, *seed*, *bleed*, *speed*, *weed*, and *feed*.

This child is deciding that *snap* has the same spelling pattern as *map*. After writing *snap* under *map* and decoding the word *snap*, she will unfold and read the sentence to be sure *snap* makes sense.

LESSONS FOR INDEPENDENCE

Now it is time to have students search in their own heads for words they know that will help them decode new words. Do not give them any known words to match. Present them with words that can be decoded based on the many known words. After you show each word, have students write that word on their paper and under it, have them write any words they know with the same spelling pattern. Ask volunteers what words they wrote with the same spelling pattern and list all the possibilities on the board. As always, when they have arrived at a pronunciation, reveal the rest of the sentence so that they can cross-check sound and meaning. Here are some sentences and the possible rhyming words to get you started. Be sure, however, to accept any words with the same spelling pattern students give you:

The huge forest fire was started by just one *spark*. (park, bark, dark)

I would like to learn to *skate*. (late, gate, Kate)

I wish I had $100.00 to *spend*. (end, send)

They put people in jail who commit a *crime*. (dime, time)

My mother makes delicious beef *stew*. (new, drew)

I want to join the Star Trek fan *club*. (rub, tub)

This child is using the known word *nine* to decode the unknown word *pine*.

Cross-Checking Meaning and Variant Spelling Patterns

Once students can look at a new word and search through their known words looking for those with the same spelling patterns, they need to learn about spelling patterns with two common pronunciations. They also need to realize that cross-checking will let them know which pronunciation works.

Write the words *know* and *show* to head one column and the words *how* and *now* to head another column. Help students to notice that the spelling pattern *ow* can have the sound in *know* and *show* or the sound in *how* and *now*. Write the words *food* and *good* to head two more columns and help students notice that the *ood* spelling pattern can be pronounced both ways. Have students head their papers just as you have headed the board.

Tell students that you will show them a word that ends in *ow* or *ood*. They should decide which pronunciation the word probably has and write it in the appropriate column. After each word is written, reveal the sentence and have the students see if their pronunciation makes sense. Some possible sentences:

When you get bigger, you *grow*.

A big black bird is a *crow*.

An animal that gives milk is a *cow*.

A farmer uses a *plow*.

When it is cold, it may *snow*.

Some houses are made of *wood*.

The teacher was in a good *mood*.

My coat has a big *hood*.

You may want to do another lesson in which you use words that have two different pronunciations. Head the board and have the students head their papers with the words, *now*, *show* and *bread*, *bead*. Show them sentences such as the following and help them to see you can't tell which pronunciation to use until you read the rest of the sentence. Students should learn that "the bad news is that in English, there is not a perfect match between spelling patterns and pronunciations. The good news is that using what you know about spelling patterns and checking to see that what you read makes sense will almost always work!"

The dancer came out and took a *bow*.

He shot the arrow from his *bow*.

My favorite team was in the *lead*.

The part of the pencil that writes is the *lead*.

I like to *read*.

This is the best book I ever *read*.

By working with word families and using words they know to match spelling patterns and figure out new words, most children eventually figure out that they can spell words by thinking of words that rhyme. A few lessons in doing this help speed the development of this useful spelling strategy.

Head the board (and have students head their papers) with three words students know that have many rhyming words—but that don't have another common spelling pattern. For this lesson, we will use the known words *but*, *bug*, and *club*.

Tell the children that they can often spell words if they think about a word they know that rhymes with the word they want to spell:

If I wanted to spell *rub*, I would think about what word I knew that *rub* rhymed with. Do *rub* and *but* rhyme? Do *rub* and *bug* rhyme? Do *rub* and *club* rhyme? Yes, *rub* and *club* rhyme. I will *start* rub with the letter *r* and then spell it like *club*.

Write *rub* under *club* on your chart and have students write it under *club* on their papers.

Continue to call out words and compare them to *but*, *bug*, and *club* to see which they rhyme with. Have students decide what letter or letters they should begin the word with and then write the word under the word that rhymes and has the same spelling pattern. Some words you might use are:

hub	plug	rug	rut	shut
chug	tub	tug	hug	nut
shrug	scrub	shrub	strut	

Do as many lessons as you feel students need. Use words that are close in sound so that students get in the habit of making the fine sound distinctions spelling requires. Use a variety of vowel sounds. If your students know the words *car*, *shark*, and *smart*, you could have them use these words as models to spell:

part	park	bark	bar	cart
dart	jar	mark	tar	lark
art	chart	spark	star	start

Hink Pinks

Hink pinks are rhyming pairs. Children love to illustrate them and to make up and solve riddles with them. Teachers love them because they help children attend to the spelling-pattern–rhyme relationship and give children a real purpose for looking for and manipulating rhyming words. Here are some to get you and your children started. Caution! Once you start hink pinking, it is hard to stop!

drab cab	rag bag	brain strain
fake snake	damp camp	thin fin
fine pine	pink drink	bright light
cold gold	long song	rude dude
book crook	broom room	last blast
brave slave	clay tray	weak beak
beast feast	red shed	free bee
hen pen	bent cent	tent rent
wet pet	nice price	crop flop
cross boss	hound sound	mouse house
stout scout	low blow	brown crown
duck truck	fudge judge	glum chum
fun run	tall wall	skunk bunk
dry fly	loose goose	

Hink pinks with riddles and illustrations by children at Clemmons Elementary School, Winston-Salem, NC.

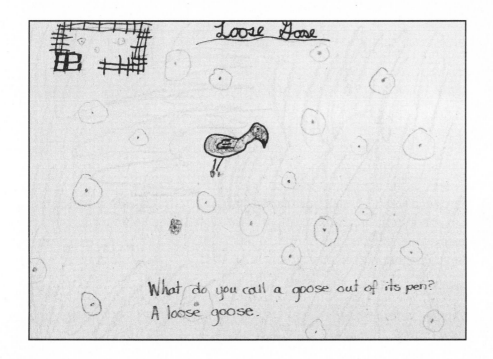

To make sure your students remember that some rhymes have two common spelling patterns, you may want to include some hink pinks such as these:

mud flood	great date	fall brawl
weak Greek	sweet treat	cheap sheep
loud crowd	rope soap	bear scare
mean queen	soup scoop	plaid pad
prune spoon	chrome foam	mole stroll

What Looks Right?

What Looks Right? is an activity through which children learn that good spelling requires visual memory and how to use their visual memory for words along with a dictionary to determine the correct spelling of a word. In English, words that have the same spelling pattern usually rhyme. If you are reading and you come to the unknown words *plight* and *trite*, you can easily figure out their pronunciation by accessing the pronunciation associated with other *ight* or *ite* words you can read and spell. The fact that there are two common spelling patterns with the same pronunciation is not a problem when you are trying to read an unfamiliar-in-print word, but it is a problem when you are trying to spell it. If you were writing and trying to spell *trite* or *plight*, they could as easily be spelled t-r-i-g-h-t and p-l-i-t-e. The only way to know which is the correct spelling is to write it one way and see if it "looks right" or check your probable spelling in a dictionary. What Looks Right? is an activity to help children learn how to use these two important self-monitoring spelling strategies.

Here is a sample lesson for the *oat-ote* pattern. Using an overhead projector or the board, create two columns and head each with an *oat-ote* word most of your children can both read and spell. Have the children set up two columns on their paper to match your model:

coat   vote

Have the children pronounce and spell the words and lead them to realize that the words rhyme but have a different spelling pattern. Tell them that there are many words that rhyme with *coat* and *vote* and that you can't tell just by saying the words which spelling patterns they will have. Next, say a word that rhymes with *coat* and *vote* and write it both ways, saying, "If the word is spelled like *coat*, it will be g-o-a-t. If it is spelled like *vote*, it will be g-o-t-e." Write these two possible spellings under the appropriate word.

Tell the children to decide which one "looks right" to them and to write only the one they think is correct. As soon as each child decides which one looks right and writes it in the correct column, have each child use the dictionary to see if that spelling can be found. If the child cannot find the one that looked right, then have them look up the other possible spelling. Cross out the spelling you wrote that is not correct and continue with some more examples. For each word, again mention, "If it is spelled like *coat*, it will be g-o-a-t, but if it is spelled like *vote*, it will be g-o-t-e." Write the word both ways and have each child write it the way it looks right and then look in the dictionary to see if the word is spelled the way the child thought.

Here is what your columns of words would look like after several examples:

coat	vote
goat	~~gote~~
boat	~~bote~~
float	~~flote~~
~~noat~~	note
~~quoat~~	quote
throat	~~throte~~
bloat	~~blote~~

To make your lesson more multileveled, include some longer words in which the last syllable rhymes with *coat* and *vote*. Proceed just as before to write the word both ways and have children choose the one that looks right, write that word, and look for it in the dictionary. For the *coat-vote* lesson, here are three longer words you might use:

~~promoat~~	promote
~~devoat~~	devote
~~remoat~~	remote

Here is a lesson for the *ait-ate* pattern. Notice that several of these pairs are both words. Children should find both *gate/gait* and *plate/plait*. This is an excellent time to talk about homophones and how the dictionary can help you decide which word to use. Also notice the words written at the bottom.

Whenever we think of common words such as *great*, *eight*, *weight*, and *straight* that don't follow the pattern, we point these out to children, explaining that most—but not all—words that rhyme with *date* and *wait* are spelled a-t-e or a-i-t.

date	wait
~~bate~~	bait
fate	~~fait~~
hate	~~hait~~
skate	~~skait~~
gate	gait
plate	plait
state	~~stait~~
rebate	~~rebait~~
debate	~~debait~~
donate	~~donait~~
hibernate	~~hibernait~~

**straight eight weight great

What Looks Right? is an active every-pupil response exercise through which children can learn a variety of important concepts. Words that rhyme usually have the same spelling pattern, but sometimes there are two common spelling patterns and you have to write it and see if it looks right or use the dictionary to check your spelling. The dictionary can also help you decide which way to spell a word when there are two words that sound the same but have different spellings and meanings. What Looks Right? is a versatile strategy and can be used to help children become better spellers of longer words. Here are two lessons for the *tion/sion* and *le/el/al* patterns.

motion	pension
action	~~acsion~~
station	~~stasion~~
~~mantion~~	mansion
mention	~~mension~~
lotion	~~losion~~
nation	~~nasion~~

~~tention~~	tension
attention	~~attension~~
extention	extension
~~division~~	division
multiplication	~~multiplicasion~~
~~televition~~	television
vacation	~~vacasion~~
~~collition~~	collision

people	model	animal
~~travle~~	~~travel~~	~~traval~~
little	~~littel~~	~~littal~~
~~channle~~	channel	~~channal~~
~~locle~~	~~locel~~	local
~~equle~~	~~equel~~	equal
~~loyle~~	~~loyel~~	loyal
settle	~~settel~~	~~settal~~
poodle	~~poodel~~	~~poodal~~
bubble	~~bubbel~~	~~bubbal~~
tunnle	tunnel	~~tunnal~~
~~normle~~	~~normel~~	normal
~~generle~~	~~generel~~	general
possible	~~possibel~~	~~possibal~~
invisible	~~invisibel~~	~~invisibal~~
principle	~~principel~~	principal

While you are working with all these rhyming words is a wonderful time to have your children write some poetry. Select a poem or two your children will like, and read it to them several times. Then, have them decide which words rhyme and whether or not the rhyming words have the same spelling patterns. Using these poems as models and the rhyming words you have collected as part of your spelling pattern lessons, students can write some interesting rhyming poetry.

Word Play Books

Words are wonderful, and every child should develop a sense of wonder and delight in encountering new words and exploring their sounds and meanings! Hopefully, many of the activities described in this book will contribute to developing word wonder in children. In addition, there are numerous books which can be read aloud to children and which they can then enjoy on their own that contribute to their developing word wonder. Any list of word play books will be quickly outdated as new and more clever ones appear, but here are a few of my very favorites to get you hooked on word play books. (As you can probably guess, I am a collector of word books. If you have favorites, I would love to hear from you!)

Fredrick by Leo Lionni—The Original Word Collector!

The *Amelia Bedelia* books by Peggy Parrish demonstrate that context really matters when you are trying to puzzle out the meanings of words.

All the *Dr. Seuss* books for rhyme, but especially *There's a Wocket in my Pocket* for developing phonemic awareness, rhyme, and consonant substitution. Children love writing class books, making up other creatures that rhyme with school and outdoor things.

The Hungry Thing by Jan Slepian and Ann Seidler is another wonderful book for phonemic awareness, rhyme, and consonant substitution play. The hungry thing is a lovable monster who asks for things to eat but mixes up the initial sound. The townspeople have to figure out that he really wants cookies when he asks for "hookies" and soup with a cracker when he asks for "boup with a smacker." Children love pretending to feed The Hungry Thing foods and figuring out what he wants to eat.

One Sun: A Book of Terse Verse and *Play Day* by Bruce McMillan. These beautifully illustrated books tell a wonderful story in two-word rhymes—terse verse. After enjoying these books and brainstorming lists of rhyming words, children delight in making their own books of terse verse.

Antics by Cathi Hepworth. A special alphabet book in which a picture of an ant and a word containing the letters *a-n-t* occur on each page, beginning with Antique, featuring a very old ant; Brilliant, a very brainy-looking chemist ant; and Chant, a group of monk-like ants singing in a dark cathedral!

Books by Fred Gwynne (Simon and Schuster), especially *The King Who Rained* and *A Chocolate Moose for Dinner*.

Books by Marvin Terban (Clarion), especially *The Dove Dove*—a delightful book with excellent examples of words that are spelled the same but pronounced differently—and *Eight Ate: A Feast of Homonym Riddles*.

Riddle books by Giulio Maestro (Clarion), especially *What's a Frank Frank?*

Joke books—especially *101 School Jokes* by Lisa Eisenber and Katy Hall (Scholastic) and *1,000 Knock Knock Jokes for Kids* (Ward Lock).

Here are three wonderful tongue twister books:

The Biggest Tongue Twister Book in the World (Gyles Brandeth; Sterling, 1978).

Alphabet Annie Announces an All-American Album (Susan Purviance and Marcia O'Shell; Houghton Mifflin, 1988).

A Twister of Twists, A Tangler of Tongues (Alvin Schwartz; Harper & Row, 1972).

Reading and Writing

It seems appropriate as we come to the end of this long chapter to remind you that none of these activities will do any good if children are not reading and writing. Remember that many children figure out on their own, through their reading and writing, the discussed strategies for spelling and decoding. The activities in this chapter cannot replace reading and writing. Nor can we just assume that reading and writing will take place—sometime. What the activities in this chapter can do is heighten children's awareness of words and accelerate the development of their understandings about letters and sounds.

As children are reading and writing, they will find useful the strategies learned through cross-checking, word families, making words, and spelling-pattern activities. You can promote the integration of these strate gies in reading and writing by the ways you respond to oral reading and by encouraging invented spelling.

Responding to Oral Reading

Most of the reading children do should be silent reading, where the focus is on understanding and enjoying what they read. It is also helpful and fun for children to have times when they read aloud. Young children like to read aloud; moreover, as they are reading aloud, teachers can evaluate how (or if?) they are using their strategies and can coach them in the appropriate use.

When children read aloud, they are inevitably going to make errors (called mistakes or miscues depending on your point of view). It is these errors that allow teachers a "window on the mind" of the reader. It is in responding to these errors that teachers have a chance to coach children into strategic reading. Some suggestions for making oral reading an enjoyable and profitable endeavor:

I. HAVE CHILDREN READ SILENTLY BEFORE READING ORALLY.

Making sure that silent reading for comprehension precedes oral reading will ensure that students do not lose track of the fact that reading is first and foremost to understand and react to the meaning of the printed words. Young children who are just beginning to read should also read material to themselves first before reading it orally. When beginning readers read, however, it is seldom silent. They don't yet know how to think the words in their minds, and their reading to themselves can be described as "mumble" or "whisper" reading.

2. ORAL READING SHOULD BE WITH MATERIAL THAT IS FAIRLY EASY.

Material that students read orally should be easy enough that they will make no more than five errors per hundred words read. If the average sentence length is seven words, this would be no more than one error every three sentences. It is very important that children not make too many errors because their ability to cross-check drops dramatically when they are making so many errors that they can't make sense of it.

3. CHILDREN SHOULD NEVER CORRECT THE READER'S ERROR.

Allowing students to correct errors inhibits the reader's ability to self-correct and forces the reader to try for "word-perfect reading." Although it might seem that striving for word-perfect reading would be a worthy goal, it is not, because it would keep our eyes from moving efficiently as we read.

When we read, our eyes move across the line of print in little jumps. The eyes then stop and look at the words. The average reader can see about 12 letters at a time—one large word, two medium words, or three small words. When our eyes stop, they can see only the letters they have stopped on. The following letters are not visible until the eyes move forward and stop once again. Once our eyes have moved forward, we can't see the words we saw during the last stop. As we read orally, our eyes move out ahead of our voice. This is how we can read with expression because the intonation and emphasis we give to a particular word can only be determined when we have seen the words that follow it. The space between where our eyes are and where our voice is is our eye-voice span. Fluent readers reading easy material have an eye-voice span of five to six words.

Good readers read with expression because their voice is trailing their eyes. When they say a particular word, their eyes are no longer on that word but rather several words down the line. This explains a phenomenon experienced by all good readers. They make small, non-meaning-changing errors when they read orally. They read "can't" when the actual printed words were *can not*. They read "car" when the actual printed word was *automobile*. Non-meaning-changing errors are a sign of good reading! They indicate that the eyes are ahead of the voice, using the succeeding words in the sentence to confirm the meaning, pronunciation, and expression given to previous words. The reader who says, "car," for *automobile* must have correctly recognized or decoded *automobile*, or that reader could not have substituted the synonym *car*. When the reader says "car," the word *automobile* can no longer be seen because the eyes have moved on.

Good readers make small non-meaning-changing errors because their eyes are not right on the words they are saying. If other children are allowed to follow along while the oral reader reads, they will interrupt the reader to point out these errors. If children are allowed to correct a reader's non-meaning-changing errors (and it is almost impossible to stop them short of gagging them), children learn that when reading orally, you should keep your eyes right on the very word you are saying! Too much oral reading with each error corrected by the children or the teacher will result in children not developing the eye-voice span all good fluent readers have.

Since gagging all the listeners would surely be misinterpreted by parents and is probably unsanitary, a simpler solution is to have all the children not reading put their finger in their books and close them! When one child is reading the others should not be "following along" the words. Rather, they should be listening to the reader read and "following along the meaning."

4. IGNORE ERRORS THAT DON'T CHANGE MEANING.

Of course, since you recognize small, non-meaning-changing errors as a sign of good eye-voice span, you will grit your teeth and ignore them!

5. WHEN THE READER MAKES A MEANING-CHANGING ERROR, WAIT!

Stifle the urge to stop and correct the reader immediately. Rather, wait until the reader finishes the sentence or paragraph. What follows the error is often the information the reader needs in order to self-correct. Students who self-correct errors based on subsequent words read should be praised because they are demonstrating their use of cross-checking while reading.

6. IF WAITING DOESN'T WORK, GIVE SUSTAINING FEEDBACK.

If the reader continues on after making a meaning-changing error, the teacher should stop the reader by saying something like:

> **Wait a minute. That didn't make sense. You read, "Then the magician stubbled and fell." What does that mean?**

The teacher has now reinforced a major understanding all readers must use if they are to decode words well. The word must have the right letters and make sense. The letters in "stubbled" are very close to the letters in *stumbled* but "stubbled" does not make sense. The teacher should then pause and see if the reader can find a way to fix it. If so, the teacher should say,

> **Yes, "stumbled" makes sense. Good. Continue reading.**

If not, the teacher should say something like:

> **Look at the word you called "stubbled." What word do you know that looks like that and is something people often do before they fall?**

If that does not help the teacher might continue by pointing out the *m* before the *b*, or by suggesting a known rhyming word, such as *crumbled* or *tumbled*.

Oral reading provides the "teachable moment"—a time for teachers to help students use the sense of what they are reading and the letter-sound relationships they know. When teachers respond to an error by waiting until a meaningful juncture is reached and responding first with a question, such as "Did that make sense?", children focus more on meaning and begin to correct their own errors. The rest of the reading group hears how the teacher responds to the error. As they listen, they learn how they should use "sense" and decoding skills as they are actually reading. Feedback that encourages readers to self-correct and monitor their reading sends a "you can do it" message.

Encouraging Invented Spelling

When young children write, their ideas are expressed in all the words they can say. Because it takes a long time to master English spelling, children will naturally write many words they haven't yet learned to spell. Children who are allowed and encouraged to "spell it so you can read it," write longer and better first drafts than children who only write words they know how to spell.

In addition to the obvious benefits invented spelling holds for writing, there are clear benefits for reading. Listen to a child who is trying to spell a word. The child will say the word very slowly, trying to segment out all the sounds and figure out what letter or letters to use to represent that sound. Children who invent-spell words as they write are performing the highest level of application of phonics!

Research on invented spelling shows that children go through stages from which you can clearly determine what they are learning about letters and sounds (Henderson, 1990). A child trying to spell the word *boat* might first just represent it with a *b*. Later that same word might be represented with a *bt*. Next, a vowel appears and *boat* is written *bot*. Finally, you see the conventionally spelled *boat* or the other possibilities, such as *bote*, and you know that the child is learning and using sophisticated knowledge about our alphabetic language.

When children are writing their first drafts, encourage them: "Say the word and write down the letters you hear yourself saying," or "Spell it the way it looks right and it will be fine as long as you can read it." In addition to acceptance and encouragement, you can give guidance to "help them along" with invented spelling! In fact, the making-words, word-families, and spelling-pattern lessons go a long way to support children's movement toward conventional spelling. There are two other activities you might do to help children feel comfortable and secure with invented spelling and move them along toward conventional spelling.

WATCH ME

Alfreda Furnas describes this technique in Jane Hansen's marvelously insightful book *Breaking Ground* (1985). She used it with her kindergarten children, but I think it would be equally appropriate for older children who aren't sure how you invent-spell!

Furnas explains that she used the overhead projector and that she began by drawing a picture. Since she is not an artist, drawing was quite difficult

Hy ant pat it is grat to be,
In my now haws my now.
Scool is grat i fek kevin.
Wal liyk goen Thar bi i haf.
To go naw irp to see you,
Soon good bi·

 The mawtin we klim.
        mountain   climb

Hi, Aunt Pat. It is great to be in my new house.
My new school is great. I think Kevin will like
going there. Bye. I have to go now. I hope
to see you soon. Goodbye.

(Writing Sample)

(John now puts periods
at the end of every line
insted of each word as
he used to)

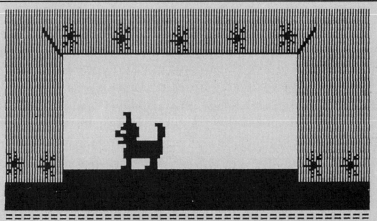

Yasd day my dad got me and my tow
bruther a dog. He is a vey vey nie dog.
He is bran and wit. He woz bon deceber
4th. Heather Hamby

Yesterday my dad got me and my two
brothers a dog. He is a very, very nice dog
He is brown and white. He was born December 4th.

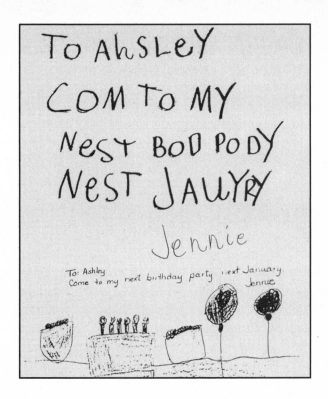

A teacher's model of how you invent-spell along with an illustration and the conventional spelling.

but she feels (and I agree) that children are more willing to take risks at things they are not good at, such as drawing and spelling, if we show them we can do things imperfectly!

After she drew the picture, she wrote a sentence in invented spelling (*Ys-trda I kt mi frst krab.*) across the top, sounding out the words and writing the letters for the most prominent sounds. She explained that she was writing the way most children wrote when they began. Then, she wrote the same sentence (*Yesterday I caught my first crab.*) in conventional spelling along the bottom and explained that this was the kind of writing adults would do and the kind children would find in books.

Next, it was the children's turn. They drew and wrote with crayons on large drawing paper. As they finished, the teacher talked to each about what they had drawn and written and then wrote a sentence or two in conventional spelling at the bottom of each paper.

CLASS INVENTION

Imagine that the whole class is going to write on the same topic—something you have been studying in science or social studies, perhaps. Make sure that everyone has a small piece of scratch paper and then have children suggest words they might need as they write about the topic. When a child suggests a word, have everyone say the word slowly and write a possible spelling on the scratch paper. When children have their individual possible spellings written, call on children to tell you how you might spell the word. Get several possibilities and write them on the board. Accept all spellings and make statements that show children their inventions are appreciated. Here are some possibilities for the words *ocean*, *vacation*, *beach* and *dunes*:

oshn	vakan	bej	doonz
ojn	vashun	beesh	dounes
oshun	vacashun	beech	doones
ocshen	vakashn	beach	donz

Once several possibilities for each word are recorded, point out to children that these are all "words you could read," their goal when getting their first-draft ideas down. Tell children that if this is a piece they want to publish, you or someone else will help them fix the spelling so that everyone can read it. Finish the lesson by writing the conventional spelling above each column and talking about when spellings were closest to the conventional spelling. (If anyone gives you the correct spelling during the invention process, accept this without comment and point it out only when you write the conventional spelling. Also, call on everyone to add to the inventions on the board and don't always call on your prize spellers!)

Dangers of Invented Spelling

Teachers who don't want children to invent spellings are usually afraid that if children invent-spell the words wrong and write them that way many times, they will learn the wrong spellings. They point to common misspellings, such as *thay* for *they*, *becuz* for *because*, and *frend* for *friend*, which often persist through the elementary grades.

This brings us back to the basic contradiction in our alphabetic language. Most words can be read and spelled correctly once you learn the basic spelling patterns that make up our language. But the most common words are the least regular! Because you must write these common words often and because you can't predict the spelling of many of them, the danger of children practicing them wrong so many times that they learn them wrong is real!

Research on invented spelling shows us that children who are reading, writing, and noticing how spelling patterns work will move through stages toward conventional spelling (Henderson, 1990). Since they don't write most words very frequently, they are not apt to fixate on an early and incorrect invented spelling. But, the common, irregular words that get written frequently may present a problem. In the next chapter, however, we discuss activities that help children learn the conventional spelling for these words and develop independent decoding and spelling skills to read and write words one can't decode or invent.

References

Adams, M. J. (1990). *Beginning to Read*. Cambridge, MA: MIT Press.

Bear, D. B., Invernizzi, M., and Templeton, S. (1995). *Words Their Way: A Developmental Approach to Phonics, Spelling and Vocabulary, K-8*. New York: Macmillan/Merrill.

Cunningham, P. M., and Hall, D. P. (1994). *Making Words*. Carthage, IL: Good Apple.

Cunningham, P. M., and Cunningham, J. W. (1992). "Making Words: Enhancing the Invented Spelling-Decoding Connection." *The Reading Teacher*, *46*, 106–107.

Hansen, J. (1985). *Breaking Ground*. Portsmouth, NH: Heinemann.

Henderson, E. (1990). *Teaching Spelling*. Boston: Houghton Mifflin.

Treiman, R. (1988). "The Role of Intrasyllabic Units in Learning to Read and Spell." In P. Gough (ed.), *Learning to Read*. Hillsdale, NJ: Erlbaum Associates.

3

High-Frequency Words

There are some words you don't want students to have to decode while reading, or invent the spelling of while writing—the frequently occurring words in our language. Of all the words we read and write, it is estimated that approximately 50 percent is accounted for by 100 highly frequent words (Fry, Fountoukidis, and Polk, 1985). These words include:

the   and   to   said   you   he   it   in   was   they

As soon as possible, children should learn to read and write these words, for two reasons.

When children at an early age learn to recognize and automatically spell the most frequently occurring words, all their attention is freed for decoding and spelling less-frequent words and, more important, for processing meaning. As you learned in the last chapter, stopping to figure out a new word while reading, or stopping to say the word slowly and figure out how you might spell it while writing, requires time and mental energy. In fact, stopping to think about a new word takes your attention away from meaning. Psychologists explain that we all have limited attention spans, sometimes called short-term memory. Short-term memory is the place that holds words or other bits of information. The short-term memory span for most people is about seven bits or seven words. When we read, we hold the words in short-term memory until we have enough words to make meaning from them. Meaning can then go into long-term memory. Thus, we make meaning from the words stored in short-term memory and send that meaning to long-term memory. This frees up all our short-term memory space for more words, and the process continues. So it goes, until we need our short-term memory space for something else—like searching through our known word store for a word with the same spelling pattern, or figuring out a word that begins with the right letters and makes sense in the sentence, or slowly saying a word we want to write and writing down the letters we hear.

Decoding or inventing the spelling of a new word takes all our short-term memory space; in fact, when this decoding or inventing process begins, all words already read or written and stored in short-term memory are dumped out (into the garbage disposal, I think!). This dumping explains why, once the word is decoded or invented, we must quickly reread any prior words in that sentence so that we may put them in short-term memory again. It also explains why children who have to decode many words often don't know what they have read after they read it! Their short-term memory space keeps getting preempted for decoding tasks and they can't reread each sentence over and over. So, they never get enough words in short-term memory from which to make meaning to put in long-term memory. All their attention is required for figuring out words, and there is no capacity for putting together meaning.

The second reason we do not want children to decode or invent-spell these words is that many of the most frequent words are not pronounced or spelled in predictable ways: if *the* were pronounced like other words with the same spelling pattern, it would rhyme with *he, me,* and *be; to* would rhyme with *go, no,* and *so; said* would rhyme with *maid* and *paid;* also, *was* would be spelled w-u-z and *they,* t-h-a-y.

As indicated before, the way we pronounce words changes with use. The words used most often are, of course, the words whose pronunciation has changed the most. In most cases, pronunciation shifts to an "easier" pronunciation. It is quicker and easier to get your tongue in position to say "the" in the usual way than it is to make it rhyme with *he, me,* and *we.* "Said" takes longer to say if you make it rhyme with *paid* and *maid.* Children should learn to read and spell the most frequently occurring words because these are the words they will read and write over and over. Many of them cannot be decoded, and if you invent the spelling, you will invent it wrong.

Teaching High-Frequency Words

Teaching the frequently used word is not an easy task. Most of the words are functional, connecting, abstract words that have no meaning in and of themselves. *There* is the opposite of *here* but if you move across the room, there becomes here! How do you explain, demonstrate, or otherwise make sense of words like *of, for,* and *from?* In addition to the problems these words create by having no concrete meaning, many of the frequently occurring words share the same letters. Besides the often confused *of, for,* and *from* and the reversible words *on/no, was/saw,* beginners are always confusing the *th* and the *w* words:

there	their	this	that
them	then	these	those
what	want	went	when
were	where	will	with

Teachers complain that despite constant drill, many children seem to learn these words one day and forget them the next!

What kind of activities can we provide to ensure that all children will learn to read and write these critical words? The most important factor to consider in teaching the highly frequent words seems to be the meaning—or, more specifically, the lack of meaning—factor.

In Chapter One, we discussed learning letter names and how children who knew some concrete words that contained the letters remembered the letters better because they had associated the letters with the already-known words. Associative learning is always more permanent than rote learning. Since these frequent words have no meaning in and of themselves, we must help the children associate them with something meaningful. To introduce the word *of,* for example, we might have pictures of a piece of pie, a can of Coke, and a box of cookies. These pictures would be labeled *a piece of cake, a can of Coke, a box of cookies* with the word *of* underlined. Next, the children would think of other things they like to eat and drink with the word *of,* such as a glass of milk, a bowl of soup, a piece of bubble gum. The labeled pictures would then be displayed to help students associate meaning with this abstract word.

After an abstract word is associated with meaning, there must be practice with that word. This practice can take many forms; but it should not consist solely of looking at the word and saying it. Not all children are good visual learners. Many children need to do something in order to learn something.

Chanting the spelling of words and writing the words provide children with auditory and kinesthetic routes to learning and remembering abstract words.

Once the children can associate meaning with a word such as *of* and have practiced *of* enough times to be able to read it and spell it, it is time to introduce one of the words with which *of* is often confused, such as *for*. You might simply extend the picture posters already made for *of* by attaching another piece of paper to each and writing the word for and the name of one of the children in your class. Underline the *for* and your posters now look like this:

a piece *of* pie <u>for</u> Tomas

a can *of* Coke <u>for</u> Patrick

a box *of* cookies <u>for</u> Tammy

Have children name foods and tell who they are for; then provide chanting and writing practice with both the words *for* and *of*.

When *of* and *for* are firmly associated and can be read and written, teach *from*. For each difficult word, think of some picture or sentence association your children would understand. Perhaps you have some children who came to your school from other states or countries. You could make some sentence posters with sentences such as:

Billy is *from* California.

José is *from* Mexico.

The children can then associate meaning with the word *from* because they know where these two classmates come from. Then provide practice with *of, for,* and *from*.

How much meaning you have to build for words and how much practice will be required to learn this varies with the different words and for different children. In general, the more abstract a word is and the more similar-looking abstract words there are, the more association and practice will be required to learn them.

The three principles for teaching the frequently occurring word are:

1. Provide a way for students to associate meaning with the words.
2. Once meaning is associated, provide practice using a variety of learning modes.
3. If a common word has many confusable words, teach one first. As soon as that one is learned, teach another and practice both. Then, teach a third and practice all three.

High-Utility Wall Words

Teachers make their own decisions about which words to add to their word walls by observing which words children use frequently in their writing. This list is intended to be an example of the kinds of words that might be included if the word wall is to have the highest utility for the children This list has high utility in multiple ways:

It includes the most frequent words—those that make up 50 percent of the words children read and write.

There is an example word for each initial consonant—*b, c, d, f, g, h, j, k, l, m, n, p, r, s, t, v, w, y, z* (including both common sounds for *c* and *g*).

There is an example for the most common blends—*bl, br, cl, cr, dr, fl, fr, gr, pl, pr, sk, sl, sm, sn, sp, st, str,* and *tr*; the common digraphs *ch, sh, th,* and *wh*; and the two-letter combinations *ph, wr, kn,* and *qu.*

There is an example for the most common vowel spelling patterns:
at, make, rain, day, car, saw, caught
went, eat, see, her, new
in, like, night, girl, thing
not, those, coat, go, for, how, slow, out, boy, look, school
us, use, hurt
my, very

There is an example for the highest-utility phonograms (Wylie and Durrell, 1970):
ack; ail; ain; ake; ale; ame; an; ank; ap; ash; at; ate; aw; ay; eat; ell; est; ice; ick; ide; ight; ill; in; ine; ing; ink; ip; it; ock; oke; op; ore; ot; uck; ug; ump; unk.

It includes the most common contractions: *can't, didn't, don't, it's, won't,* and the most common homophones: *to, too, two; their, they're; right, write; no, know; one, won't;*

It includes words such as *favorite, teacher, school, family,* and *sister*; which young children use frequently in their writing.

Ideally, a classroom word wall would add five words per week and have about 100 to 120 words by the end of the year. This list contains 180 words, which is too many for any one word wall. In some schools, first-grade teachers pick the most frequent words for their walls. Second-grade teachers begin the year by putting up some of the first-grade words which are particularly hard to spell—*they, were, because,* and so on—and then add others.

about	fly	mother	than
after	for	my	thank
all	friend	name	that
am	from	new	the
an	fun	nice	their
and	get	night	them
animal	girl	no	then
are	give	not	there
as	go	now	they
at	good	of	they're
be	green	off	thing
because	gym	old	this
been	had	on	those
best	has	one	time
big	have	or	to
black	he	other	too
boy	her	out	trip
brother	here	over	truck
bug	him	people	two
but	his	phone	up
by	house	play	us
call	how	presents	use
can	hurt	pretty	very
can't	I	question	want
car	if	rain	was
caught	in	ride	way
children	into	right	we
city	is	run	went
clock	it	said	were
coat	it's	sale	what
come	joke	saw	when
could	jump	school	where
crash	junk	see	which
day	kick	she	who
did	know	sister	why
didn't	like	slow	will
do	line	skate	with
don't	little	small	won
down	long	snap	won't
drink	look	so	would
each	made	some	write
eat	mail	sports	you
family	make	stop	your
father	many	street	zoo
favorite	me	talk	
first	more	teacher	
		tell	

Words on the Wall

One strategy we have found particularly effective for teaching the highly frequent words is Words on the Wall (Cunningham, Moore, Cunningham, and Moore, 1989). We select four or five words each week and add them to a wall or bulletin board in the room. Sometimes these words have a picture or sentence clue and sometimes the word is displayed alone. When words are displayed alone, we make sure that they are words students have already associated meaning with or we display picture-sentence posters somewhere else until that meaning is built.

The selection of the words varies from classroom to classroom, but the selection principle is the same. We include words students will need often in their reading and writing and that are often confused with other words. First-grade teachers who are using a basal usually select some highly frequent words taught in that basal. Some teachers select their words from a high-frequency word list. Here is a sample from a first-grade classroom, halfway through the year:

A word wall example, taken from a first grade, halfway through the year.

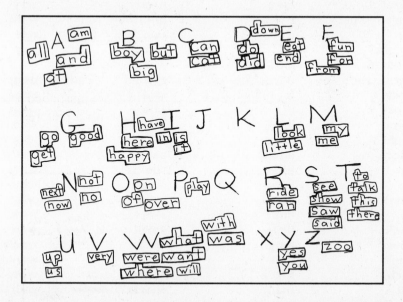

The word wall grows as the year goes on. The words are written with a thick, black-ink, permanent marker on scraps of different-colored construction paper. Words are placed on the wall alphabetically by first letter, and the first words displayed are very different from one another. When confusable words are added, we make sure they are on a different color paper from the other words they are usually confused with. Cutting around the configuration is another helpful cue to those confusable words. Children who are looking for *where* tend to distinguish it from *were* by its "*h* sticking up."

Following is a word wall used in a fourth-grade classroom. The teacher began the wall by putting up words she knew fourth graders often misspelled. She added five each week and, at the end of the third week, the word-wall looked like this:

A	*B*	*C*	*D*	*E*	*F*	*G*	*H*	*I*
again	because	come	does		from		have	
		could						

J	*K*	*L*	*M*	*N*	*O*	*P*	*Q*	*R*
					of	pretty		
						people		

S	*T*	*U*	*V*	*W*	*X*	*Y*	*Z*
said	they			was			
				were			
				where			

Word wall of a fourth-grade class after three weeks.

During these three weeks, she looked for words commonly misspelled in the children's writing and added them to the wall. The misspelled words included many homophones, and these were added with a picture or phrase clue. Here is the word wall at the end of ten weeks:

A	*B*	*C*	*D*	*E*	*F*	*G*	*H*	*I*
again	because	come	does	enough	from	guess	have	I'll
ate	by	could	deer	eight	families	grade	hear	isn't
	be	cent	dear	everybody	friend		here	
	bee	city						

J	*K*	*L*	*M*	*N*	*O*	*P*	*Q*	*R*
		let's	meat	next	of	pretty	question	right
		learn	meet	neighbor	o'clock	people		real

S	*T*	*U*	*V*	*W*	*X*	*Y*	*Z*
said	they			were		your	
sent	tomorrow			was		you're	
school				where			

The same word wall after ten weeks.

And here it is at the end of the school year. As you can see, more words from the children's writing were added to the word wall (including many contractions), and more common homophones.

The same word wall near the end of fourth grade.

Most teachers add new words each week and do at least one daily activity in which the children find, write, and chant the spelling of the words. The activity takes longer on the day you add words because you will want to take time to make sure students associate meanings with the words, and you point out how the words are different from words they are often confused with. Several ways to get at least once-daily practice with the word-wall words follow.

Clap, Chant, and Write

Have students number a sheet of scratch paper from one to five. Call out five words, putting each word in a sentence. When all five words have been written, point to the words and have the students clap and chant the spelling of the words as they correct their own papers.

On the day you add words to the word wall, call out the five new words. During the rest of the week, however, any five words from the wall can be called out. Words with which children need much practice can be called out almost every day.

The children clap and chant the spelling of each word-wall word they have written and check their own papers.

Review Rhyme with the Word Wall

Students number their paper just as they do for Clap, Chant, and Write, but they must write the word that rhymes with a word you give. Give them both a first letter and a rhyming clue:

Number one begins with a *t* and rhymes with *walk*.

Number two begins with an *m* and rhymes with *by*.

Number three begins with an *f* and rhymes with *run*.

Number four begins with an *l* and rhymes with *bike*.

Number five begins with a *g* and rhymes with *stood*.

To check the answers, you say the rhyming word and let students say the word they wrote and chant its spelling. "Number one rhymes with *walk,* what did you write?" Children respond, "talk, t-a-l-k."

The children are writing the word-wall words on their scratch paper as the teacher calls them out from the wall.

Review Endings with the Word Wall

Call your words; some of which will need endings added to them. Begin with just one ending, probably *-s*. Then do another ending, such as *-ing* or *-ed*. Then combine them so that children are listening for all the endings. Do not call out words with spelling changes until you have taught these, or give them a hint. For example:

"Having," remember that you must drop the e on "have" before adding the ending.

Add endings to some, but not all of the words you call out. Have students chant and check in the usual manner.

Review Cross-Checking with the Word Wall

To review cross-checking, tell students that they will have to decide which wall word makes sense and begins correctly. For each word, write the first letter of the word on the board. Then say a sentence, leaving out a word that begins with that letter. Students will decide which word makes sense in your sentence and write that word. Some examples:

1. Write *t* on board. Say, "The first word begins with a *t* and fits in the sentence *Paula likes to . . . on the telephone.*"

2. Write *r* on board. Say, "Number two begins with an *r* and fits in the sentence *Midge had to . . . fast to win the race.*"

3. Write *w* on board. Say, "Number three begins with a *w* and fits in the sentence *Carlos went to China . . . his father.*"

4. Write *p* on board. Say, "Number four begins with a *p* and fits in the sentence *Carol, Bobby, and Joyce are all . . .*"

5. Write *g* on board. Say, "Number five begins with a *g* and fits in the sentence *Louella and Suzette are . . . runners.*"

To check the answers, read the sentences again and have students tell you what word they wrote and chant its spelling.

Make Sentences with Word-Wall Words

Dictate a sentence or two to the children using the word-wall words. Have students listen as you say the whole sentence; then, repeat the sentence, one word at a time, giving students plenty of time to find the words on the word wall and write them. Remind children to begin their sentences with capital letters. Have days when you dictate questions, which require a question mark, and exclamatory sentences, which require an exclamation mark.

You may want to allow children to dictate the sentence. Have them prepare their sentence ahead of time and write it down so that you can check to see that all words are on the wall and that it is indeed a sentence.

Be a Mind Reader

Be a Mind Reader is a favorite word-wall activity. In this game, the teacher thinks of a word on the wall and then gives five clues to that word. Choose a word and write it on a piece of scratch paper but do not let the students see what word you have written. Have students number their scratch paper one to five and tell them that you are going to see who can read your mind and figure out which of the words on the board you are thinking of and have written on your scratch paper. Tell them you will give them five clues. By the fifth clue, everyone should guess your word, but if they read your mind they might get it before the fifth clue. For your first clue, always give the same clue: "It's one of the words on the wall." Students should write next to number one the word they think it might be. Each succeeding clue should narrow down what it can be until by clue five there is only one possible word. As you give clues, students write the word they believe it is next to each number. If succeeding clues confirm the word a student has written next to one number, the student writes that word again by the next number. Clues may include any features of the word you want students to notice. (It has more than two letters. It has less than four letters. It has an *e*. It does not have a *t*.) After clue five, show students the word you wrote on your scratch paper and say, "I know you all have the word next to number five but who has it next to number four? Three? Two? One?" Some students will have read your mind and will be pleased as punch with themselves!

1. It's one of the words on the wall.
2. It has four letters.
3. It begins with *th*.
4. The vowel is an *e*.
5. It finishes the sentence *I gave my books to* . . . .

Ruler Tap

A ruler is used for another activity. The teacher says a word and then taps out several letters in that word without saying those letters. When the tapping stops, the teacher calls on a child to finish spelling the word out loud. If the child correctly finishes spelling the word, that child gets to call out a word and tap some of the letters.

Wordo

Wordo is a variation of the ever-popular Bingo game. Children love it and don't know they are getting a lot of practice reading and writing highly frequent words! All you need to play Wordo is some photocopied sheets on which 9 or 25 blocks have been drawn in, and some small pieces of paper, or objects, for students to use to cover words as they fill in the blocks. Reproduce a good supply of these grid sheets and you are ready when the assembly program is canceled or the foreign language teacher suddenly quits!

Call on students to pick words from the wall they want included in the game. As each word is picked, students will write it on their wordo sheets in a blank block they choose, and you will write it on an index card. (Make

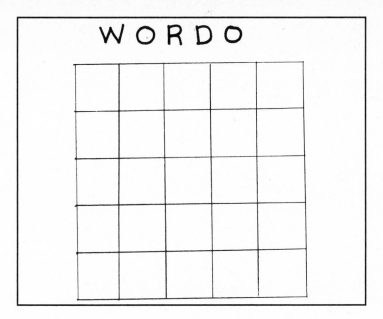

W O R D O

A blank **Wordo** sheet for older children.

W O R D O

A blank **Wordo** sheet for younger children.

sure students understand that unlike its Bingo counterpart, all children will ultimately have all the same words that are called out. Since they will have written them in different places, however, there will still be winners. Unfortunately, you can't play for a full card!)

When all students have filled up their sheets with the 9 or 25 words called out, you are ready to play. Shuffle your index cards and call the words one at a time. Have students chant the spelling of each word and then cover it with paper squares or small objects.

The first student to have a complete row covered wins Wordo. Be sure to have the winner tell you the words covered and check to see that the words have been called. Students can then clear their sheets and play again. You might let the winner become the next caller and you can play the winner's sheet. Children love watching their teachers lose!

Word Sorts

Word sorts can be done with the words on the wall or any group of words the teacher wants students to concentrate on. The purpose of word sorts is to focus student attention on the various features of the words. To do a word sort, write 10 to 15 words on large index cards and have students write these words on separate slips of paper. Have the students sort the words into different piles depending on some features certain words share. Students may sort all words with a certain number of letters, all words that begin with a certain letter or all words that have a certain letter anywhere in them.

Sometimes, the teacher tells the students the criterion on which to sort, for example, all words with an *a* in them. Other times, the teacher tells students which words to select—*boy, try, my, day*—and the students must guess how these words are all alike. In this case, these are all words that end in the letter *y*. Sorting words based on the number of letters and on the different letters and sounds represented by the letters helps students attend to those letters.

Words can also be sorted according to semantic features. Students might choose all the things or all the words that name people. Words that describe things, words that tell what you can do, words that name things found outside are just some of the many possibilities for sorting based on semantic features. Once students understand the various ways the words can be sorted, they can play the role of teacher and tell which words to choose or a criterion for sorting the words.

Commonly Used Homophones, Contractions, Compound Words, and Other Hard-to-Spell Words Often Found on Intermediate Word Walls

HOMOPHONES

ate-eight
bare-bear
be-bee
blew-blue
board-bored
brake-break
buy-by
capital-capitol
cell-sell
cent-sent
close-clothes
dear-deer
for-four
groan-grown
hear-here
heard-herd
hi-high
hole-whole
hour-our
in-inn
its-it's
knew-new
know-no
meat-meet
one-won
pail-pale
pair-pear
piece-peace
plain-plane
rap-wrap
right-write
road-rode
sail-sale
sea-see
son-sun
steal-steel
their-there-they're
threw-through

to-too-two
wait-weight
way-weigh
weak-week
wear-where
weather-whether
which-witch
who's-whose
wood-would
your-you're

CONTRACTIONS

aren't
can't
couldn't
didn't
doesn't
don't
hasn't
haven't
he's
here's
I'd
I'll
I'm
I've
isn't
let's
she's
that's
there's
wasn't
we'll
we're
we've
weren't
what's
won't
wouldn't

you'll
you've

COMMON COMPOUNDS

anyone
anything
another
baseball
basketball
football
birthday
cannot
everywhere
everyone
everything
everybody
herself
himself
itself
myself
yourself
ourselves
themselves
however
into
inside
outside
someone
something
somebody
somewhere
sometimes
maybe

NOT COMPOUNDS

a lot
no one
all right

<u>**WORDS WITH**</u>
<u>**CAPITALS**</u>
I
American
English
Mr.
Mrs.
United States
Holidays
Months
Days
States

<u>**OTHER WORDS**</u>
about
again
almost
also
already
although
always
around
beautiful
because
before
believe
business
bought
brought
city
cousin

different
earth
either
enough
especially
family
favorite
finally
first
friends
getting
government
guess
happened
laugh
machine
measure
minute
million
money
morning
mountain
nation
ocean
off
often
once
people
picture
pretty
probably

really
receive
said
scared
school
science
special
stopped
surprise
swimming
television
terrible
they
thought
tired
tomorrow
together
tried
trouble
until
usually
very
vacation
was
watch
went
were
world
wrong

Portable Word Walls

Portable word walls were invented by an enterprising remedial-reading teacher whose third graders complained that they couldn't "right good" in her room because they didn't have their word wall. Upon investigation, it was discovered that their classroom teacher had a colorful word wall and that these remedial readers depended on the wall for spelling highly frequent words as they wrote. Any thought of constructing a word wall in the remedial teacher's "room" was quickly dismissed when the teacher remembered her room was really a closet and that other teachers used this space. The problem was solved by constructing portable word walls made of file folders divided alphabetically. The classroom teacher, the remedial teacher,

A portable word wall made on a file folder.

Outside of folder

Inside of folder

G g good get girl give great	H h here had happy he how his have her help	I i is isn't if it into	J j just	K k keep know	L l little look like
M m my me man maybe many make more	N n not no now night	O o of on over off old	P p people play	Q q quick	R r read.

and the students worked together to copy all the words on the wall to the folders, using permanent markers the same color as the paper on which wall words were written. Then, each week, as five words were added to the classroom word wall, the teacher and students added them to their portable word walls. The students took their word walls to remedial reading and home for the summer. Perhaps, they even took them to fourth grade the next year!

Word Wall as Reading and Writing Aid

Once you have a word wall growing in your room, it will be evident that your students use it as they are reading and writing. You will see their eyes quickly glance to the exact spot where a word they want to write is displayed. You will hear them say things: "I need that *too;* that is the 'Me too' *too.*" or "*Where* starts with *w* and is the red word with the *h* sticking up." Even when children are reading, they will sometimes glance over to the word wall to help them remember a particularly troublesome word.

Word walls provide children with an immediately accessible dictionary for the most troublesome words. Because the words are added gradually; stay in the same spot forever; are listed alphabetically by first letter; are often made visually distinctive by different colors of paper and by cutting around the configuration; and because of the daily practice in finding, writing, and chanting these words, almost all children learn to read and spell almost all the words. Because the words you selected are words they need constantly in their reading and writing, their recognition of these words becomes automatic and their limited attention can be devoted to the less-frequent words and to constructing meaning as they read and write.

Fluency Comes from Lots of Easy Reading

Fluency is fast, expressive reading. The easiest way to imagine fluency is to remember what a nonfluent reader sounds like:

Some children read one word at a time hes—si—ta—ting and and and re—peat—ing words.

In the previous sentence, I have tried to remind you what a nonfluent reader sounds like. Every teacher has had the experience of working with children who can read most words but for whom reading is a tortured, labored word-by-word, sometimes syllable-by-syllable, process. Children who lack fluency generally only read when they have to and have not developed the automatic and immediate identification of words which lots of reading leads to. There is an almost certain prescription for developing fluency—lots of very easy reading! Knowing that easy reading is the right medicine is the easy part! Getting nonfluent readers to take that medicine is the hard part. Nonfluent readers are often older children who don't think of themselves as good readers and don't want to read the easy books they deem "baby books!"

Linda Fielding and Cathy Roller attack this "baby book attitude" head on in a 1992 *Reading Teacher* article "Making Difficult Books Accessible and Easy Books Acceptable." Among the ideas for making difficult books accessible are:

1. Provide independent reading time when children can self-select books (including nonfiction) and interact with others about what they learn from these books.

2. Read difficult books to the children.

3. Partner the children, putting a more able reader with a less able reader.

4. Provide lots of rereading opportunities because difficult material becomes easier each time it is read.

5. Precede difficult books on a topic with easier books on that topic to build background knowledge.

All these suggestions will help children read with more fluency even when the material they are reading is more difficult than it should optimally be.

Among their many practical ideas for making easy books acceptable Fielding and Roller suggest:

1. Modeling, by reading aloud, the use and enjoyment of easy books.

2. Altering purposes for easy reading by having older children read these books to younger buddies.

3. Allowing children to make tape recordings of favorite books.

4. Making the expanding world of nonfiction books readily available.

I have seen all four of these strategies successfully used and even a combination that worked like this. A fourth-grade teacher with many children still reading—not very fluently—at first- and second-grade levels decided that the children needed to do lots of easy reading. She partnered each child with a kindergartner and arranged for a weekly reading time. She then gathered up a lot of easy books, including many Dr. Seuss titles, Clifford books, and many nonfiction picture books (including alphabet books, some of which are listed in Chapter One). Across the course of a week or two, she read these books to her children and let each child choose one book to prepare to read to the kindergarten buddy. When the children had chosen their books, they practiced reading the book several times—with a partner—to the tape recorder—and finally to the teacher. By the time her children trotted down to the kindergarten—easy books proudly in hand—all the children were fluent readers of their book.

Upon their return to the fourth grade, they talked about their experience with their kindergarten buddies and whether or not their book was a good choice. The teacher made a chart on which each child listed the book read aloud that week. The following day, the teacher and the children gathered and reviewed the chart showing who had read what. The teacher also reminded them of some other books no one had chosen the first week and led them to choose their second book. The partner reading, tape-recorder reading, and reading to the teacher continued as it had for the first week except that, if a child chose a book which another child had read the previous week, that child became the "expert" on that book and read the book to or listened to the new reader read the book at least once. The second trip to the kindergarten went more smoothly than the first, and the children returned, discussed the kindergartners' responses to the books, and listed the second book they had read on the chart.

By the fourth week, the easy-reading-for-fluency program was up and running with minimal help from the teacher. Many children chose books their friend had chosen previously, and they enjoyed reading together and often tape recording the book together in preparation for performing their weekly "civic volunteer" duty!

Easy reading is essential for children to develop fluency. This easy reading can be accomplished and legitimized in a variety of ways. Another wonderful *Reading Teacher* article I recommend to anyone concerned with fluency is "The 'Curious George' Strategy for Students with Reading Problems" (Richek and McTague, 1988). In this article, the authors describe how they used assisted reading and a series of books—in this case the Curious George books—to help some second- and third-grade remedial readers develop reading fluency, confidence, and enjoyment.

Assisted reading (Hoskisson, 1975) is what it sounds like. The teacher assists a group of children through repeated readings of some text. Usually, the teacher reads the text the first time, the children chime in with known words the second time, and rereading continues as the children take over more and more of the reading. This article brings a new twist to assisted reading by using the popular Curious George series. The teacher assisted the children in reading many books in the series and as they read more and more books, most children were able to—and preferred to—do the initial reading of one of the later-used Curious George books on their own.

In addition to repeated reading and assisted reading, Choral Reading is a time-tested strategy which will help children become fluent readers. To do choral reading, most teachers begin with a piece of poetry or a chant the children are familiar with. The material for choral reading should be duplicated or put on a chart or overhead to make the print visible to everyone. Next, decide which parts everyone—the chorus—should read and which parts will make good solos, and assign parts and solos. You will need to practice the piece several times—with the readers becoming more fluent each time. Be sure to emphasize how to speak dramatically, and include some sound effects if the piece allows that. Once you have practiced several times, perform the choral reading for a group or make a video or audio tape of your performance.

All kinds of poems and chants can be used for Choral Reading. Children respond particularly well to the rhymes in Joanna Cole's *Anna Banana: 101 Jump Rope Rhymes* (1989) and to the book Cole wrote with Stephanie Calmenson, *Miss Mary Mack and Other Children's Street Rhymes* (1990). Another great source for "kid-pleasing" choral readings is Ruth Dowell's *Let's Talk!* (1986).

Fluency comes from the ability to immediately and automatically identify the most frequent words. Learning to spell these words through daily and varied practice with word-wall words promotes this fluency. The other key ingredient is lots and lots of easy reading.

Books for Easy Reading

There are an increasing number of easy-reading collections available for beginning readers. Primary classrooms should be well stocked with such materials. Some of these sets are listed below.

Little Celebrations. Scott Foresman (Glenview, IL), 75 titles, K–1.

The Sunshine Series: Fiction. The Wright Group (Bothell, WA), 116 titles, K–1 levels, with big books.

The Sunshine Series: Science. The Wright Group (Bothell, WA), 24 titles, K–1 levels, with big books.

Look-Look-Books. Goldencraft (Chicago), 27 titles, 1–2 levels.

Literacy 2000. Rigby (Crystal Lake, IL), 55 titles, K–1 levels.

I Can Read Collection. Scott Foresman (Glenview, IL), 31 titles, 1–2 levels.

Step into Reading. Random House (New York), 76 titles, 1–3 levels.

Banners. Scholastic (New York), 120 titles, 1–2 levels, with big books.

Rookie Readers. Children's Press (Chicago), 56 titles.

New Way Readers. Steck-Vaughn-Raintree (Austin, TX), 142 titles, K–2 levels, with tapes.

SERIES BOOKS

Series books, such as those listed below are wonderful materials for easy reading. Series books are easier than a variety of books because the reader builds up a store of information about the characters and the author's style that make the books more predictable. Kids often devour series books not just because they are easier but because they like them!

N. Bridwell's *Clifford, the Big Red Dog series,* Scholastic

M. Rey's *Curious George,* Scholastic

Mercer Mayer's *Little Critters,* Scholastic

Pat Reilly Giff's *The Polk Street School Kids,* Dell

Judy Delton's *Pee Wee Scouts,* Dell

Else Minarik's *Little Bear* books, Harper & Row

Cynthia Rylant's *Henry and Mudge* books, Macmillan

James Marshall's *George and Martha* books, Sandpiper

References

Cunningham, P. M., Moore, S. A., Cunningham, J. W., and Moore, D. W. (1989). *Reading in Elementary Classrooms: Strategies and Observations.* New York: Longman.

Fielding, L., and Roller, C. (1992). "Making Difficult Books Accessible and Easy Books Acceptable." *The Reading Teacher*, *45*, 678–685.

Fry, E., Fountoukidis, D.L., and Polk, J. K. (1985). *The New Reading Teacher's Book of Lists.* Englewood Cliffs, NJ: Prentice-Hall.

Hoskisson, K. (1975). "The Many Faces of Assisted Reading." *Elementary English*, *52*, 653–659.

Richek, M. A., and McTague, B. K. (1988). "The 'Curious George' Strategy for Students with Reading Problems." *The Reading Teacher*, *42*, 220–226.

4

Big Words

Big, or long, words present special decoding problems for children. Most of the words children read are one-syllable words. Big words are seen fairly infrequently, but when they do occur, they are often the words that tell most of the story. Here is a paragraph from *Sports Illustrated for Kids* (July, 1989, p. 14) in which all the words of two or more syllables have been deleted and replaced with a blank:

Few things feel as good as _____ the _____ of your _____ _____
_____. You _____ the thrill of _____ him face to face, and you get
to take home a _____ _____.

As you can see, it is impossible to make sense of even simple paragraphs intended for children when you can't read any of the big words. Some of these big words are quite easy to decode because they consist of a one-syllable word with a common ending added or two common one-syllable words forming a compound word. The paragraph from the preceding example is now repeated with these easily decodable two-syllable words replaced:

Few things feel as good as *getting* the _____ of your _____ *baseball* player. You _____ the thrill of *meeting* him face to face, and you get to take home a _____ _____.

You can now discern that this paragraph is about baseball and has to do with meeting players, but you are still not getting much meaning from this paragraph. Perhaps you could use your strategy of cross-checking meaning with the consonant letters to figure out the missing big words:

Few things feel as good as getting the --t–gr–ph of your f–v–r–t– baseball player. You –xp–r–––nc– the thrill of meeting him face to face, and you get to take home a v–l––bl– m–m–nt–.

Although it is possible to figure out the words: *autograph, favorite, experience, valuable,* and *memento,* few children can do it. (I tested this with three 12-year-olds who figured out *autograph, favorite,* and *experience* but were stumped by *valuable* and *memento.*) When there are many big words, you have to keep rereading to figure them out, and you need some of them before you can get the others. This process is slow and cumbersome and it would be impossible to sustain this kind of effort throughout the entire article.

Then, how do readers figure out big words that they don't immediately recognize and that carry most of the meaning of what they are reading? It is not absolutely clear how readers perform this feat; nevertheless, it is probable that they use the same analogy strategy used with one-syllable words. When faced with an unfamiliar-in-print big word, good readers will search through their store of known words in order to find other words with the "same parts in the same places."

Autograph may be seen: "like *automobile* at the beginning and like *paragraph* at the end." *Favorite* may be seen as "beginning with *favor,* and then it has to be *favorite* to sound right in the sentence." *Experience* is more difficult for most children. They might decode it, however, by seeing that it begins like *experiment* and ends like *difference. Valuable* is *value* with the common ending, *-able. Memento* is not too hard to decode but many children might not have it in their listening vocabularies and might pronounce it with the first syllable accented—mee-men-to. If they know enough big words that end in *t-o* such as *lotto* and *tomato* and *Pluto,* they will probably pronounce the last syllable correctly. If not they will probably pronounce it like the known word *to.*

The strategies required to decode big words seem to be the same strategies required to decode one-syllable words. The reader must stop and look at all the letters in the word, simultaneously searching through the store of known words for words with the same patterns. The reader must then cross-check the pronunciation achieved with the meaning of what is being read. With polysyllabic words, however, there are the additional requirements of knowing where to break the word and how to put it back together again (Cunningham, 1978).

Do you remember being taught to decode polysyllabic words by learning a set of syllabication and accent rules? Do you remember learning to "divide between two consonants unless the consonants are a digraph or a blend"? Did you learn that "the next to the last syllable is often accented"?

The syllabication and accent rules were well intended. Good readers do see polysyllabic words in chunks and they do know which syllable to accent, once they figure out the word. But, good readers do not seem to do this by using rules (Canney and Schreiner, 1977). Rather, they look for chunks based on words they already know. Often—as in *autograph, favorite,* and *experience*—some chunks (*auto, favor, experi*) may be larger than a syllable. Accent is usually determined not by applying accent rules but by pronouncing a word different ways until one way sounds correct. If the word is not in your listening vocabulary, you can't be sure about which syllable to accent.

Many children who can read almost any one-syllable word have difficulty decoding big words. Often, their first strategy upon encountering a big word is to "guess it" and their second strategy is to "skip it." Guessing it is better than skipping it, and you often can guess correctly if the context is rich and you use your consonant knowledge. But guessing the word based on a few letters and the context does not require you to study all the letters in the word; thus, you are unlikely to add the word to your store of known words. The reader who guessed *experience* by using the consonant letters in the paragraph above might not recognize that same word in a much diminished context. For example: *Experience is the best teacher.*

Skipping the big words is obviously not a good strategy. There is no chance of adding that word to the store of known words, and comprehension is greatly diminished when the big words that are carrying most of the meaning are skipped.

Because big words have their own letter-sound pattern predictabilities, readers need a store of known big words. Certain letter combinations (*tion, sion, tial,* etc.) are completely predictable in big words and nonexistent in one-syllable words. In big words, the sound of certain spelling patterns is totally determined by the position in the word. Notice the difference in the way you pronounce the *t-o* at the beginning and end of *tomato* and the *l-e* at the beginning and end of *legible.*

In order to use known words to figure out big words, you must know some big words. Not only must you be able to read some big words, but you must also be able to spell those big words. You can't recognize *experience* as beginning like *experiment* and ending like *difference* unless you can both read and spell *experiment* and *difference.* The requirement that you be able to spell some big words along with the tendency of readers to guess or skip any word of more than seven letters may partially explain why so many children experience problems reading their content-area texts.

In this chapter, you learn how to help children build a store of big words they can read and spell and how to help them use words they know to figure out unknown big words. The first section of this chapter describes strategies for helping children build a store of big words. The activities described in the remainder of the chapter are for helping children learn to look closely at all the letters of new words, compare these new words to known words, and cross-check meaning. None of these activities is a prerequisite to any of the others; so you can pick and choose and intermix them for variety as well as to ensure you are meeting the different learning styles and preferences of all your children.

Building a Big Word Store

Content-Word Boards

There are numerous opportunities to help students build a store of big words they can read and spell. The first place to look is in your content-area subjects. Science and social studies are the natural hiding places of many of these words. Helping children learn to read and spell some of them will serve the dual purposes of building a store of big words and helping children read and write about that subject. You may want to reserve a bulletin board for your "Big Weather Words" or "Big Washington, D.C., Words," Here are some word boards for these two topics.

Weather words displayed on a content-word board. The words are added gradually, and children enjoy learning such big words.

Weather
temperature   climate
Satellites   forecasting
                prediction
thunderstorm hurricane
    atmosphere tornado
latitude lightning pressure
longitude precipitation
                    snowfall
    humidity   rainfall
        greenhouse moisture
weather vane   blizzard
    barometer rainbow
meteorologist typhoon

As you can see, there are numerous big words students will need as they read and write about the weather and Washington, D.C. Notice how many of the common polysyllabic patterns are illustrated by the words listed under just these two topics. Students who can read and write *nation* and *constitution* have known words which end in *-tion*. The word *temperature* provides a clue for the many big words that end in *-ture*.

Washington, D. C.

nation   government
president   senators
Congress   Constitution
representatives   federal
museum   Capital
monuments   Capitol
national   sculpture
Congressional
tourists   embassies
demonstrations
inauguration

**A Washington, D.C.,
big-word board.**

Add a few big words each day and use the word-wall activities described in Chapter Three to review them and focus attention on them. Unlike the crucial words in Chapter Three which need to be kept visible and reviewed all year, you probably will want to take these words down and begin a new word board as you begin new science or social studies units.

Collect Big Words from Reading

Send students hunting, in their reading, for big words related to something you are learning about. Have a topic for each week and hang a chart somewhere. Label the chart and help students list a few words to get started. Then have students add to this chart as they find words from their reading. Have them initial words they add so they can receive accolades at the end of the day when the list is read. You may want to specify a minimum of length for the words—perhaps seven or eight letters. Some teachers start a new chart each week but then keep the old ones around for several more weeks constantly encouraging students to add to them. Some charts and the words collected for the topics follow:

Occupations

physician	physical therapist	fisherman
meteorologist	custodian	decorator
veterinarian	principal	mechanic
undertaker	professor	construction worker
secretary	electrician	waitress

Big Words for Said

answered	confessed	promised
whispered	murmured	reminded
suggested	explained	muttered
stammered	exclaimed	pleaded
snickered	bragged	stuttered
requested		

Big Words Describing People

unhappy	curious	tremendous
delighted	famished	nervous
thrilled	patient	brilliant
overjoyed	miserable	mysterious
frightened	lovable	hilarious
paralyzed	astonished	

Sending students hunting for big words that fit a topic has the serendipitous effect of changing your students' mindsets toward big words. Instead of wanting to quickly guess or skip a big word, children will stop and try to figure it out and then see if it can be added to any of the big-word charts.

Big Word of the Day

Each day, students hunt all day for a big word which they think is the best big word! Each student can find one each day. The student writes that word on a "ballot" along with his or her initials and places it in the big word voting box. At the end of each day, the teacher pulls out all the words and reads them to the class. The student who "nominated" the word can give a short speech telling why it is such an interesting, important, useful, or otherwise wonderful word. The class then votes, and the chosen word is written on an index card and added to the "Word of the Day" bulletin board. Here is a Word of the Day board from one classroom.

```
Big, Gigantic, Enormous Words
      refrigerator       computer
           microwave
     motorcycle      restaurant
        athletic    limousine
   motorcycle    television
      ridiculous   stupidity
                  dynamite
    Olympics        intelligent
   hurricane
            gymnastics
  entertainment   obsession
      Catastrophe
    Superstar    blockbuster
```

Words chosen by some fifth graders as their favorite big words.

How Did I Choose?

How Did I Choose? is a word-sorting activity in which words are selected based on some feature, and the children have to guess what that feature is. It is a wonderful review activity for any of the big words collected in your room, or for reviewing big words. To do the activity, write the words on large index cards. Some describing words that might be used are:

dependable	flexible	optimistic
pessimistic	reliable	responsible
cooperative	creative	imaginative
impulsive	repulsive	reflective
immature	impatient	malicious
suspicious	considerate	intelligent
unemotional	unobservant	confident
insecure	insensitive	innocent

Put the words along the chalk ledge or in a pocket chart, one at a time, as you have pupils pronounce them and talk about meanings. Tell students that you will choose some words because you are thinking of a particular feature all these words share. It could be a letter or a word part or a meaning relationship. Their job is to guess what you were thinking of that made you choose some words and not others.

Begin by taking *impulsive, impatient, imaginative,* and *immature* and putting them to one side. Ask, "Why did I take *impulsive, impatient, imaginative,* and *immature* and not the others?" Students should easily guess that these four words begin with *i-m* and none of the others do.

Next, take *creative, insecure, immature, flexible,* and *innocent.* It may take students longer to see that you were choosing words with eight letters. If they guess something that is not true, point out why it couldn't be: "If I had been taking words with *i,* I would also have had to take *imaginative, unemotional,* and others."

Then, take *dependable, responsible, reliable, creative, and imaginative.* Students should guess that you chose words with similar meanings.

Continue by taking *insecure, confident, optimistic, pessimistic, impulsive, reflective, insensitive, and considerate.* Students should guess that you chose words with opposite meanings.

Next, take words that contain a specific letter, *e* for example. Then take *pessimistic, cooperative, immature, intelligent, innocent.* If students have difficulty figuring out the feature all these words have in common that the others don't have, underline the *ss* in *pessimistic,* the *oo* in *cooperative,* and the other double letters; then listen to the students groan: "These are the words with double letters!"

You may want to let a student choose based on some feature and let the others guess on what feature that student is choosing. Have the student whisper to you the feature and words he or she will choose to ensure a success.

There are endless possibilities for choosing. Students enjoy this game; moreover, it is excellent for training them to think and allowing them to review the salient features of their words.

RIVET—A Vocabulary Introduction Activity

RIVET is a prereading activity I created one day while sitting in the back of a fourth-grade classroom watching one of my student teachers trying to introduce some vocabulary words to her students. The vocabulary she was introducing was important to the story, and many students needed to focus on these words and their meanings. The student teacher was diligently writing the words on the board and having students use them in sentences and trying to help the students access meanings and relate them to each other. Unfortunately, the students were not particularly interested in the words, and their attention was marginal at best. When the words had been introduced and the students began to silently read the selection, I quietly approached some of the less-able readers and helped them find the introduced words in their text and had them read the sentences containing these words to me. It was no surprise that for the children who didn't already know the pronunciation and meaning for these words, they hadn't learned them from the vocabulary introduction. RIVET was conceived that day and has since saved many a student teacher from the dreaded experience of having taught some words that no one seemed to have learned!

Activating children's prior knowledge and getting them to make predictions before they read is one sure way to increase the involvement and comprehension of most children. RIVET is an activity designed to accomplish this critical prereading goal. To prepare for a RIVET text introduction, read the selection and pick six to eight important words—with a particular emphasis on polysyllabic words and important names.

Begin the activity by writing numbers and drawing lines on the board to indicate how many letters each word has. Have the students draw the same number of lines on a piece of scratch paper. Your board and their paper at the beginning of the RIVET activity would look like this:

1. _ _ _ _ _ _ _ _ _ _
2. _ _ _ _ _ _ _ _ _
3. _ _ _ _ _ _ _ _ _
4. _ _ _ _ _ _ _ _
5. _ _ _ _ _ _   _ _ _ _ _ _ _ _ _
6. _ _ _ _ _ _ _ _
7. _ _ _ _ _ _ _ _ _

Fill in the letters to the first word one at a time. Have the students write them as you do and encourage them to guess as soon as they think they know the word. Most students could not guess the word when the board looks like this:

1. une _ _ _ _ _ _ _
2. _ _ _ _ _ _ _ _ _
3. _ _ _ _ _ _ _ _ _
4. _ _ _ _ _ _ _ _
5. _ _ _ _ _ _   _ _ _ _ _ _ _ _ _
6. _ _ _ _ _ _ _ _
7. _ _ _ _ _ _ _ _ _

But many will guess with a few more letters:

1. unexpe _ _ _ _ _

Once someone has guessed the correct word, ask him or her to help you finish spelling it and write it on the board as students write it on their papers. Begin writing the letters—pausing for just a second after writing each—of the second word:

1. unexpected
2. am _ _ _ _ _ _ _
3. _ _ _ _ _ _ _ _ _

4. _ _ _ _ _ _ _ _ _

5. _ _ _ _ _ _   _ _ _ _ _ _ _ _ _

6. _ _ _ _ _ _ _ _ _

7. _ _ _ _ _ _ _ _ _

The attention of all the students is generally riveted (thus the name RIVET) to each added letter and with a few more letters many students will guess the word.

  1. unexpected — — — —

  2. ambul _ _ _ _

If they are right, have them help you finish spelling it. If they give you an incorrect guess, just continue writing letters until someone guesses the correct word. Continue in this fashion until all the word have been completely written and correctly guessed. Here is what the board and student's papers would look like when all words were introduced:

  1. unexpected

  2. ambulance

  3. emergency

  4. Elizabeth

  5. golden retriever

  6. hurricane

  7. terrifying

Now, have the students use these words to predict some of the events in the story. Encourage divergent predictions by asking questions which lead them to consider alternative possibilities. One child may say,

"A girl named Elizabeth was hurt in a hurricane."

Accept that response but ask a question such as:

Does Elizabeth have to be a girl character in the story?

Help the students think about the fact that hurricanes are given names and perhaps this hurricane is named Elizabeth. Students may also realize that Elizabeth could be the golden retriever! Ask these kind of questions even if the first prediction was correct. Prediction is a powerful prereading activity not because the predictions are always right but because the process of predicting requires that students access whatever prior knowledge they have and bring it to bear on the selection. After the students have read the selection, use the key words to review their predictions and talk about what actually happened. Be sure to let the students know that you are not just interested in "the right answer." You may want to say something like, "That didn't happen, but it could have, and it might have made a more interesting story."

Familiar Spelling Patterns

As students progress in acquiring a store of big words they can read and spell, they need to have their attention directed to the spelling patterns commonly found in big words. The activities described here will lead children to look for patterns in words. *Making Big Words* helps students see that the way they put many letters together determines the word they get. *Modeling* is a way for teachers and children to "think aloud" about what they do when they come to a big unknown word. Finally, *Mystery Word Match* allows students to practice recombining familiar chunks in a game format.

Making Big Words

Lessons on Making Words were described in Chapter Two. Similar lessons can be done with big words and older children. When doing a Making Big Words lesson (Cunningham and Hall, 1994), print the letters needed at the top of a piece of paper (vowels first, then consonants in alphabetical order so as not to give away the big word). Then leave spaces for children to write and sort words on the remainder of the paper. The children cut apart the letters from the top of the sheet and manipulate these to make words. They write the words they make in the boxes.

Here is the sheet all the children started with. After cutting the letters from the top, they manipulated them to make words and wrote them in the boxes. The second sheet shows the words one child came up with in the allotted five to six minutes.

| e | e | o | o | l | l | n | s | t | w | y |

Making Big Words sheet from which children cut apart letters.

to	low	eyes
too	lowest	style
two	lost	tell
news	lose	sell
snow	loose	well
snowy	loosely	yell
slow	lonely	yellow
slowly	only	Yellowstone
town	sweet	swell

Sheet with words one child came up with.

Here are several Making Big Words lessons in which the big word comes from a topic being studied. The children cut the letters from the top of the sheet and then write the words they can make in the boxes.

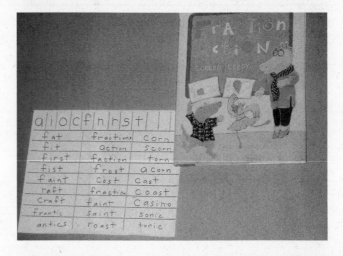

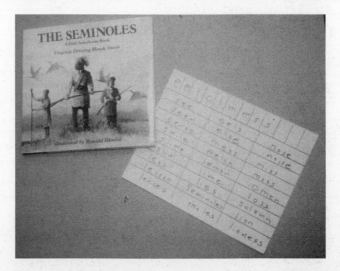

When the children have had five to six minutes to make words and write them on their paper, let them each tell you one word they made. They spell the word and if it is spelled correctly and can be made from the letters they have, write it on an index card and put it in the pocket chart.

Once the children have contributed all the words they made, the words in the pocket chart are sorted for patterns with the teacher and students suggesting various ways to sort them. Just as in Making Words, the focus of Making Big Words lessons is on the spelling patterns words share.

Modeling: How to Figure Out a Big Word

When you model, you show someone how to do something. In real life, we use modeling constantly to teach skills. We would not think of explaining how to ride a bike. Rather, we demonstrate and talk about what we are doing as the learner watches what we do and listens to our explanation. Vocabulary introduction is a good place to model for students how you figure out the pronunciation of a word. The word should be shown in a sentence context so that students are reminded that words must have the right letters in the right places and make sense. Following is an example of how you might model for students one way to decode *entertainment:*

"I am going to write a sentence on the board that has a big word in it. I will 'think aloud' how I might figure out this one. After I show you how I decode this one, I will let several of you model how you would decode other words."

Write on the board: *Different people like different kinds of entertainment.*

"Now I am going to read up to the big word and tell you how I might figure it out. If you figure out the word before I do, please don't say it and ruin my performance!"

Read the sentence and stop when you get to *entertainment.*

"This is a long word but I can probably figure it out if I think of some other words I know."

Cover all but *enter.*

"The first chunk is a word I know—*enter.* The second chunk is like container and maintain."

Write *container* and *maintain* on the board, underlining the <u>tain</u>.

"Finally, I know the last chunk is like *argument* and *moment.*"

Write *argument* and *moment* on the board, underlining the <u>ment</u>.

"Now, I will put the chunks together: *enter-tain-ment.* Yes, that's a word I know and it makes sense in the sentence because my brother and I certainly are different and we don't like the same TV shows or movies or anything."

Since English is not a language in which letters or chunks have only one sound, you might also write the word *mountain* on the board, underlining the *tain* and pointing out to students that the letters *tain* also commonly have the sound you hear at the end of *mountain*. Have students try pronouncing *entertainment* with the different sounds for the *tain* chunk. Point out that it sounds right and makes a word you know when you use the sound of *tain* you know from *maintain* and *container*. Remind students that if they use the probable sound of letters together with the sense of what they are reading, they can figure out many more words than if they just pay attention to the letter sounds, ignoring what makes sense, or if they just guess something that makes sense, ignoring the letter sounds.

As you can see from this example, when you model, you talk about what your brain is thinking. Students listen and watch, learning, thus, how to apply their decoding skills to actual words. Next, write several more sentences with big words and let students volunteer to model how they might decode the word. As students model, help them to put their thoughts into words and be sure they read the sentence to combine the sense of the sentence with the letter-sounds clues they are using.

To get students both to look for big words in their reading and to think about how they decode them, give each student a large index card. Tell students that they should be on the lookout for one big word that they think would be a new word for most of the students in the class. Demonstrate for students how to fold their index card in half if the big word is at the beginning or end of the sentence in which they find it, or in thirds if the big word is in the middle of the sentence. Let's look at this example for a word found at the end of a sentence. On the bottom half of the index card is the word *precision*. On the top half, folded out of view, is the rest of the sentence:

A folded index card used to model how to decode *precision* and then, with the card unfolded, check to make sure it makes sense in the sentence.

Bonnie is so dedicated that she

refused

the invitation to the white house.

A folded index card used to model how to decode *refused*.

She executed the high dive with

Show just the word first and think aloud something like,

"This is a new word but it begins with the *pre* chunk I know and ends with c-i-s-i-o-n, which is also the way *decision* ends. I will try those two chunks. *Precision*. Now I will reread the sentence to cross-check."

Reveal the sentence and say something like,

"Yes, that makes sense. She did the high dive precisely right!"

Now, in another example the big word is in the middle of the sentence. (The index card is folded in thirds; the word *refused* is in the middle; the top third says, *Bonnie is so dedicated that she;* the bottom third says, *the invitation to the White House.*) You would show the word (*refused*) first and explain how you figured it out. Then, reveal and read the rest of the sentence to confirm meaning.

For this activity, it is best to take your example from a variety of real sources, including magazine and newspaper articles and, whenever possible, to show students the source. (These two sentences came from a newspaper sports page.) Students will then see the need for using their decoding skills in "real-world" materials. Encourage students to find their big words in real-world sources too. The index-card/find-a-stumper strategy make a fairly good homework assignment one night each week. Students enjoy finding big words and explaining how they figured them out!

Mystery Word Match

Mystery Word Match is a game in which students try to guess a mystery word, which has parts like two or three clue words. To play, divide the students into two groups. The word is worth ten points. With each "no" answer to a question, the turn shifts to the other team and a point is subtracted. Write each sentence and clue words on the board. Read the sentence, saying "blank" for the mystery word. Pronounce the clue words and have the students pronounce them. Students ask, "Does the mystery word begin like (one of the clue words)? End like. . . ? Have a middle like. . . ?" Here is an example:

The restaurant was __ __ __ __ __ __ __ __ __.

        dependable

        excitement

        impulsive

TEACHER: The mystery word has nine letters. Listen while I read the sentence. The clue words are *dependable, excitement, and impulsive.* Say them after me. Maria's team won the toss. They can go first. The mystery word is worth ten points.

MARIA'S TEAM MEMBER: Does the word begin like *impulsive?*

TEACHER: No, it does not. Joe's team for nine points.

JOE'S TEAM MEMBER: Does the word end like *impulsive?*

TEACHER: Yes, it does. (Write *sive* on the last four lines.) Go again.

JOE'S TEAM MEMBER: Does the word begin like *dependable?*

TEACHER: No, it does not. Maria's team, eight points.

MARIA'S TEAM MEMBER: Does the word have a middle like *dependable?*

TEACHER: Good! (Write *pen* on the appropriate lines.) Go again.

MARIA'S TEAM MEMBER: Does the word begin like *excitement?*

TEACHER: Yes it does. (Write *ex.*) The team may confer and name the word.

Maria's team confers and triumphantly pronounces *expensive.*

Teacher records eight points for Maria's team.

The game continues with more sentences. Some mystery words have only two clue words, one for what the mystery word begins like and another for what it ends like. This will seem easy but it is good for helping students see chunks larger than a syllable. A few more examples:

She wrote a _ _ _ _ _ _ _ _ _ _ _.
       (composure, confrontation, invisible)

She wanted to make a good _ _ _ _ _ _ _ _ _ _.
       (depression, impulsive)

He had an _ _ _ _ _ _ _ _ _.
       (optimistic, confrontation, generously)

The senate passed the _ _ _ _ _ _ _ _ _ _ _.
       (resolution, legislature)

He was in a _ _ _ _ _ _ _ _ _ _ _ _ _.
       (sensational, confident, overtime)

We will all have to _ _ _ _ _ _ _ _ _.
       (revitalize, economical)

The answers are much more apparent to you than they are to children. (In case they are not readily apparent, the mystery words are: *composition, impression, operation, legislation, conversational,* and *economize.*)

Two cautions I must give you about Mystery Word Match. First, be sure that the clue words have the same letters and sound and that the part of the clue word you want to use is in the same position in the mystery word. Because the sounds of letters in big words change based on where those letters are in the word, we want children to use word-segment position as an important clue when they are searching through their word store for words with "the same parts in the same places." If your students enjoy Mystery Word Match, you should probably invest in a rhyming dictionary, which will let you quickly locate clue words for middle and ending chunks.

The second caution is needed because, in the heat of competition, someone occasionally blurts out the answer out of turn. This spoils the game for everyone. You can nip this in the bud, however, if you make it clear that if anyone says the answer out of turn, the other team automatically gets the points. You must then support your words with the appropriate action the first time this happens. Some children hold their hands over their mouths to control themselves once they have figured it out!

Morphemes

Morphemes include prefixes, suffixes, and roots, which are meaningful parts of words. Many big words are only small words with lots of added morphemes. *International* is easily decoded if you recognize the common prefix *inter-* and the common suffix, *-al.*

Often, morpheme instruction focuses solely on prefixes or suffixes as they provide clues to the meanings of words. Students are taught that *inter-* means between or among, and they use this to figure out that *international* means between nations. Unfortunately, prefixes such as *inter-* also begin many words such as *interfere, interruption,* and *internal;* in the latter, there is a "between or among" meaning to the *inter-* prefix, but the rest of the word is not a known root word. Most students could not figure out the meaning of *interfere* by combining their knowledge of the Latin root *-fere* with the meaning of between or among associated with *inter-.* Because in so many words students cannot use prefix-suffix knowledge to help them figure out a meaning, they often decide that "this prefix-suffix stuff doesn't work" and they then stop paying attention to these morphemes.

Instruction in using morphemes as clues to the meanings of words can be useful. Teachers should point out the meaning of *inter-* in *international* and *uni-* in *unilateral* whenever it will add to students' vocabulary knowledge or vocabulary learning strategies. Instruction in using morphemes can also be helpful to students when the morphemes function simply as decoding cues. Most students know the meanings of the words *interruption* and *interfere.* They, therefore, do not need to use *inter-* to get the meanings of the words. They do, however, need to see *inter-* as a common prefix in many words so that they can correctly pronounce the *inter-* chunk and then use other words they know to figure out the rest of an unknown word. Learning about morphemes will help children decode big words and in some cases give clues to the meanings of words.

The following are descriptions of a generic modeling lesson that can be used to introduce big words with many morphemes and specific activities to do with compound words, prefixes, suffixes, and root words.

Modeling: How Morphemes Help You Decode Big Words

An opportune time to teach students to use morphemic clues for pronouncing words is when words are being introduced. Science and social studies present many opportunities for teachers to point out how looking for familiar morphemes helps you pronounce words and sometimes helps you figure out meanings for words. The next example shows what a teacher might do and say to introduce the word *international.*

Write on the board or overhead transparency: *The thinning of the ozone layer is an international problem.*

"Today, we are going to look at a big word that is really just a little word with a prefix added to the beginning and a suffix added to the end."

Underline <u>nation</u>.

"Who can tell me this word? Yes, that's the word *nation,* and we know *nation* is another word for *country.* Now, let's look at the prefix that comes before *nation.*"

Underline <u>inter</u>.

"This prefix is *inter.* You probably know *inter* from words like *interrupt* and *internal.* Now, let's look at what follows *inter* and *nation.*"

Underline <u>al</u>.

"You know *al* from many words, such as *unusual* and *critical.*"

Write *unusual* and *critical* and underline the <u>al</u>.

"Listen as I pronounce this part of the word."

Underline and pronounce <u>national</u>.

"Notice how the pronunciation of *nation* changes when we put *a-l* on it. Now let's put all the parts together and pronounce the word *inter nation al.*" Let's read the sentence and make sure *international* makes sense."

Have the sentence read and confirm that ozone thinning is indeed a problem for many nations to solve.

"You can figure out the pronunciation of many big words if you look for common prefixes, such as *inter,* common root words, such as *nation,* and common suffixes, such as *al.*

"In addition to helping you figure out the pronunciation of a word, prefixes and suffixes sometimes help you know what the word means or where in a sentence we can use the word. The word *nation* names a thing. When we describe a nation, we add the suffix *al* and have *national.* The prefix *inter* often means "between or among." Something that is *international* is between many nations. The Olympics are the best example of an *international* sports event."

This sample lesson for introducing the word *international* demonstrates how a teacher can help students see and use morphemes to decode polysyllabic words. As in the sample lesson for *entertainment,* the teacher points out words students might know that have the same chunks—in this case, morphemes. In addition, meaning clues yielded by the morphemes are provided whenever appropriate.

Although this lesson in and of itself will not teach students to look for and use morphemic clues in accessing pronunciation and meaning, imagine the cumulative effect that is possible if just one word were introduced like this each day. The word, of course, would be one students needed to read or write, and the introduction would take just a few minutes. Those few minutes, however, multiplied times 180 days and 180 words would ensure that children were adding many big words to their big word store and were learning to look for and use morphemic clues.

Compound Words

Compound words are a good beginning point to help children see that sometimes you can figure out the pronunciation and meaning of big words by looking for known small words in the unknown big word. Compound words abound in English, and children catch on to decoding them very quickly. Thus, they get some instant success, which may help them overcome bigwordphobia. As always, it is crucial that children cross-check meaning with pronunciation. Children who are reading for meaning will never pronounce *father* as "fat her" or *washer* as "was her."

Whereas the pronunciation of a compound word can almost always be derived by pronouncing the two separate words together, the meaning is not always derivable by combining the two words. Students should learn that many big words are just little words combined and that by looking closely at all the letters (as opposed to guessing or skipping the word), they can figure out the pronunciation and sometimes the meaning of many big words.

COMBINING CONTENT AND COMPOUNDS

You will find many opportunities to point out compound words as students are reading and writing in science and social studies. Many animal names are compound words. Point out three or four of these to your students (*blackbird, rattlesnake, woodpecker, starfish*) and begin a chart of "Compound Animals." Encourage children to see how many they can find. As more compound animals are added, talk about how the two words are combined to describe something about the animal. Just for fun, create new compound words for new animals. How about a greenbird, a wigglesnake, a woodstabber, and a moonfish? Have students pick a new compound animal, write about its habits, and use some art media to create their animal.

There are many other science and social studies topics that have lots of compound words you can alert students to. You just have to be on the lookout for compounds; then, send your students to hunt. Weather, too, is a unit that has many compound words. Many of these include the root words *sun, rain, snow,* or *storm.* You might want to point out a couple of compounds with each of these roots and have students look for others. Students may enjoy combining the words in different ways and imagining what they would be: If we can have a rainstorm, a thunderstorm, a snowstorm, and a windstorm, what would a sunstorm be? Here are some weather compounds to get you started.

sundown	raincoat	snowman	thunderstorm
sunlight	raindrop	snowball	snowstorm
sunset	rainbow	snowflake	windstorm
sunstroke	rainmaker	snowsuit	
sunflower		snowplow	
sunroom			

COMPOUNDS FOR SOMEBODY, ANYBODY, EVERYBODY

Compounds that begin with *some, any,* and *every* are the most frequently used compounds in English, and as such, children should learn to read and spell them. You may want to start a word board and add some words each day. Add the triplets first, then the pairs, and finally, a few single ones. Have children chant the spelling and write the words. Once you get the list finished, you may want to point out that there are some words you use together that are not compounds (every time; any day). Add these to the list, if you like, but be sure to put a big space between them and have the children chant them "e-v-e-r-y space t-i-m-e" to emphasize that they are not written as compounds.

anybody	somebody	everybody
anyone	someone	everyone
anything	something	everything
anyplace	someplace	everyplace
anywhere	somewhere	everywhere
anytime	sometime	
anyhow	somehow	
	someday	everyday
	sometimes	
	somewhat	
anyway		

You may want to bring in some old recordings or lead the children in singing such old favorites as "Everybody Loves Somebody Sometime," "You're Nobody 'til Somebody Loves You," "You're Everything to Me," and "Somewhere" (*West Side Story*), just to show them how relevant these compounds are to the real world!

ROOTS WITH MANY COMPOUNDS

There are some words in our language from which many compounds have been made. Write a word such as *fire* on the board ten times. Have children simultaneously write it on a piece of paper. Give children two minutes to add words to *fire* which they think might make compound words. When the two minutes are up, have them check dictionaries to see which words are really compounds. Help them see how the dictionary uses different symbols to show which words are written as compounds and which word pairs are written separately. Put those compound words they have listed on the board and add any they find interesting when looking through the dictionary.

Some children may enjoy illustrating these compound words. For fun, you may have them illustrate what some of the compounds are not: an airline is not a line in the air; a firehouse is not a house on fire; an airdrop is not when you drop air.

Some *fire, air,* and *sea* compounds to get you started:

fireman	airport	seaport
firewood	airmail	seashell
fireworks	airline	seaside
fireplace	airplane	seashore
fireside	airlift	seaweed
fireproof	airtight	seaplane
firehouse	airdrop	seasick
fireplug	airman	seafood
firetrap	aircraft	seagull
firebird	airborne	seacoast
firearm	airsick	seaquake
fireball		

There are some root words that make many compounds with other words added before and after them. You may want to have your students make compounds with words such as *ball, light,* and *back.* Write the word *ball* ten times in the middle of your chart paper and have them do the same on their paper. Give them two minutes to make as many compounds as they can by adding a word before or after *ball.* Use the dictionary to check and add. Illustrations both real and strange (a lighthouse floating away, a room filled to the brim with balls) are fun for these words too.

ballgame	lighthouse	backpack
ballpark	lightweight	backyard
ballroom	lighthearted	background
ballplayer	lightyear	backfire
hardball	lightheaded	backboard
softball	flashlight	backache
baseball	headlight	backbone
football	nightlight	backbreaking
basketball	sunlight	fullback
handball	moonlight	quarterback
volleyball		halfback

Teaching Common Prefixes and Suffixes

Thousands of common English words begin and end with prefixes and suffixes. The prefixes *un-, re-,* and *in-* are the most common. Common suffixes include *-y, -ly, -er, -ness, -tion/-sion* and *-able/-ible.* Children need to look for these prefixes and suffixes as clues to the pronunciation and, sometimes, to the meaning of words.

SAMPLE PREFIX ACTIVITIES

Write nine words that begin with *re-* on index cards. Include three words in which *re-* means "back," three words in which *re-* means "again," and three words in which *re-* is just the first syllable and has no apparent meaning. Use words for which your students are apt to have meanings:

rebound	**redo**	**record**
return	**replay**	**refuse**
replace	**rework**	**reveal**

Place these words randomly along the chalk ledge, have them pronounced and ask students what "chunk" the words all have in common. Once students notice that they all begin with *r-e,* arrange the words in three columns on the board and tell the students to think about why you have put together *rebound, return,* and *replace; redo, replay,* and *rework;* and *record, refuse,* and *reveal.* If students need help, tell them that for one column of *re-* words, you can put the word *again* in place of the *re-* and still have the meaning of the word. Explain that for another column, you can put the word *back* in place of *re-.* Once students have figured out in which column the *re-* means "back" and in which *re-* means "again," label these columns, *back* and *again.* Help students see that when you refuse something, you don't fuse it back or fuse it again. Do the same with *record* and *reveal.*

Have students set up their own papers in three columns, the first two headed by *back* and *again* and the last not headed, and write the words written on the board. Then say some other *re-* words and have students write them in the column they think they belong in. As each word is written, ask someone where they wrote it and how they spelled it. Write it in the appropriate column on the board. Conclude the activity by having all the *re-* words read and replacing the *re-* with *back* or *again* when appropriate. Help students summarize that sometimes *re-* means "back," sometimes *re-* means "again," and sometimes *re-* is just the first chunk of the word. Some additional words you might use are:

reusable	retire	retreat	rewind
recall	respond	remote	responsible
recoil	rewrite	refund	relief

A similar activity could be done for words that begin with *un-*. Include words in which *un-* means "not" or "the opposite of," in which *uni-* means "one," and in which the *un-* is just the first chunk. Use words your students are apt to know to start the list:

unfair	unicorn	under
unpack	united	uncle
unarmed	uniform	undertaker

And use other words you may want students to decide about:

unfortunate	unstable	unicycle	unique
union	unlimited	unequal	understand
unknown	unusual	unspoken	untangle
unlock	unhealthy	unclear	underwear

In another activity, you might pair the prefix *in-* meaning "not" with the prefix *inter-* meaning "between." Set up the activity as before with examples for the *not* meaning, the *between* meaning, and words in which *in-* is just the first chunk. Then have pupils listen to words and write them in the appropriate columns:

inactive	international	industry
insane	intermix	infant
ineffective	intersection	infest
infinite	interchange	insect
indefinite	interact	innocent
independent	intermingle	instrument
inconvenient	interweave	internal
intolerant	intercontinental	interesting

You might conclude this activity by writing these words on the board and helping students see that *in-* meaning "not," sometimes becomes *il-*, *im-*, or *ir-* to match the first letter in the root word:

illegal	impossible	irregular
illiterate	impolite	irrational
illegible	immature	irresponsible

Two other prefixes, *dis-* and *non-,* also commonly mean "not" or "the opposite of." Here are some words you might use for showing students the *dis-* and *non-* chunks, and how sometimes they signal an opposite relationship:

disobey	disaster	nonfiction
disarm	dispatch	nonviolent
discontinue	dispense	nonprofit
disapprove	distinguished	nonbreakable
discover	distant	nonstandard
disappear	distress	nonsupport

Note that there are no common words that start with *non-* in which *non-* does not signal an opposite relationship. So, teach it because it is so dependable!

There are some prefixes in English that when paired signal opposite relationships: we can undereat or overeat; our ancestors were proslavery or antislavery; we can go to a pregame party or a postgame party. Following is an activity for *pre-* and *post-* that you can adopt to teach opposite prefixes, such as *over-, under-; pro-, anti-.*

Write the words *preconference, prepare, postconference, postpone* on the board. Underline the *pre* or *post* in each word. Help students see that *pre-* often means "before": the preconference games are played before the beginning of the conference; you prepare for something before you do it. *Post-* often means "after": the postconference games are played after the conference game; when you postpone something, you put it off until later.

Tell students that when they see a word containing *pre-* or *post-* whose meaning they do not know, they should try to figure out a meaning related to *before* or *after* and see if that meaning makes sense in the sentence they are reading.

Divide your board or transparency into three columns and label them *root, pre-* and *post-*. Have students do the same on their paper. Write some words that will make words with *pre-, post-,* or both under *root*. Have students write the word under *root* and then combine the root with *pre-, post-,* or both and write it in the appropriate columns. Talk about the meanings of the real words and about what words would mean if they existed: "Is it possible to be postmature?" "Could you possibly postdetermine something?"

```
root            pre-        post-
test
mature
election
script
trial
season
paid
game
establish
determine
caution
teen
```

Regardless of which prefixes you choose to focus on, your message to students should be the same: "Prefixes are chunks at the front of words, which have predictable pronunciations. Look for them and depend on them to help you chunk and pronounce new words. Sometimes, they also give you meaning clues. If you are unsure about the meaning of a word, see if a common meaning for the prefix can help."

In addition to the prefixes included above, next is a list of other common prefixes, their meanings, and a couple of examples and nonexamples for each.

Prefix	Meaning	Example	Nonexample
mis-	bad wrong	misbehave misdeal	miscellaneous mistletoe
sub-	under part of	subway subcommittee	subsist substance
trans-	across	transcontinental transatlantic	translate transparent
super-	more than great	superman superpower	superintendent
semi-	half	semifinal semiannual	seminar
mid-	middle	midcourt midnight	midget

SAMPLE SUFFIX ACTIVITIES

Suffixes, like prefixes, are predictable indicators of pronunciation and sometimes signal a meaning relationship. The meaning signaled by suffixes, however, is not usually a meaning change, but rather a change in how and in what position the word can be used in the sentence. *Compose* is what you do. The *composer* is the person doing it. A *composition* is what you have once you have composed. Students need to become aware of how words change when they are signaling different relationships. They also need to realize that there are slight pronunciation changes in root words when suffixes are added. Some sample activities for the most common suffixes follow.

To teach *-er,* write words on index cards that demonstrate the someone or something who does something and comparative meanings as well as some words that just end in *-er.* Place the words randomly along the chalk ledge and have students notice that the words all end in *-er.* Next, arrange the words in four columns, as shown subsequently, and help students see that column-one words are all people who do something, column-two words are things that do something, column-three words mean "more," and column-four words are those in which *er* is just the last chunk:

reporter	computer	fatter	cover
photographer	pointer	skinnier	never
teacher	heater	greater	master

Label the first three columns *People Who Do, Things That Do,* and *More.* Do not label the last column. Have pupils set up papers in four columns, labeling and listing the words just as you have done on the board. Call out some *-er* words and have students write them in the column they think they belong in. Then, have students spell each word and tell you which column to put the word in. Remind students of spelling rules—changing *y* to *i,* doubling letters—as needed. Some *-er* words you might use are:

after	richer	fighter	winner
winter	under	heavier	air conditioner
murderer	manager	copier	dish washer
runner	diaper	writer	typewriter

A common suffix that is always pronounced the same way and that sometimes signals a change from doing to the thing done is *-ion.* Students make this shift easily in their speech and need to recognize that the same shift occurs in reading and writing. Write -*tion* words on index cards, some of which have a related "doing" word and some of which don't. After students notice that the words all end in -*tion* and that the -*tion* chunk is pronounced the same, divide the words to form two columns on the board. For example:

collection	nation
election	fraction
attraction	vacation

Help students see that when you collect coins, you have a coin *collection;* we elect leaders during an *election;* and you have an *attraction* for someone you are attracted to. In *nation, fraction,* and *vacation,* the -*tion* is pronounced the same but the meaning of the word is not obvious by looking at the root word. Have students set up their papers in the usual way and call out words for students to decide which group they fit with. Be sure to have students spell words as you write them on the board and talk about the meaning relationships where appropriate. Here are some starters:

traction	subtraction	construction	rejection
auction	expedition	tradition	interruption
mention	action	pollution	correction

And some -*sion* words you could use in a similar activity are:

confusion	invasion	vision	provision
extension	suspension	passion	expression
collision	mission	tension	explosion

You may also want to do the common suffixes -*able/-ible.* There are many words in which the -*able* or -*ible* relates the word back to a root word and shows a meaning relationship: a dress that is in fashion is *fashionable;* a coat that can be reversed is *reversible.* There are fewer words in which the -*able* does not signal a meaning relationship: *miserable* is one example. There are other examples in which the -*able* is pronounced to rhyme with *table.* In many -*ible* words (*visible, tangible, incorrigible*), the relationship is only clear if you are a Latin scholar. The following are some possibilities for -*able* and -*ible:*

fashionable	comfortable	reasonable
miserable	stable	huggable
enjoyable	washable	cable
incomparable	incapable	lovable
eligible	forcible	audible
digestible	flexible	convertible
possible	collapsible	sensible
responsible	compatible	incorruptible

Additionally, you might want to do the following activity in which you combine several of the suffixes to show how root words are changed as they are added.

Write the words *compute, computer, computation, and computable* on the board. Pronounce the words as you underline the *comput-* in each word. Help students to see that when you *compute* something, you count it, or calculate it, or figure it out. Thus, a *computer* is a machine that computes. Then, *computation* is what you do as you compute. And, something that can be computed is *computable*.

Set up your board, or overhead transparency and have students set up their paper the same way. Help students decide if a new word can be added that ends in *-er, -able,* or *-ation*. Some words can make new words with all three but some only add one or two suffixes. Have them write each new word they can make in the appropriate column.

As each word is written, have students spell it and talk about how the meaning is related to the root word meaning:

```
                      -er      -able      -ation
present
import
adore
invite
restore
export
quote
interpret
```

Two suffixes, *-ful* and *-less,* often do add meanings to words to which they are attached. Begin with some pairs for which your students are apt to have meanings:

careful	careless
hopeful	hopeless
harmful	harmless
helpful	helpless

Give students a list of words and have them decide which words make new words by adding *-ful, -less,* or both. Talk about the meanings of the words they made. Point out that *-ful/-less* pairs often have opposite meanings, but not always. Help students with spelling changes as necessary. Some words that make new words with *-ful* or *-less,* or both:

law	rest	resent	delight	cheer
doubt	plenty	disgrace	power	spoon
pain	skill	faith	plate	shame
stain	motion	taste	sense	ground
time	arm	life	name	speech

A list of other common suffixes follows, with examples and nonexamples for each:

Suffix	Meaning	Example	Nonexample
-ly	in that manner	happily steadily briefly	assembly family ugly
-or	person who or thing which	inspector generator	mirror horror
-ist	person	scientist artist	consist exist

Suffix		Meaning	Example	Nonexample
-ance			tolerance ignorance	balance romance
-ence		state of act of	violence obedience	silence sequence
-ment			development argument	document moment
-ness			laziness blindness	witness harness
-ant			tolerant ignorant	assistant elephant
-ent			violent confident	incident urgent
-al		related to	comical memorial	animal initial
-ive			creative active	motive adjective
-ous			nervous malicious	curious delicious

Teaching Common Root Words

So far, we have talked about working from prefixes and suffixes back to the root word. Some children find it exciting to see how many different words they can read and understand from just one root word. Students need to learn that the pronunciation of a root word often changes slightly as prefixes and suffixes are added. They also need to learn that the root sometimes helps them to come up with meanings. Some sample root-word activities are described next.

Write the word *play* on the board. Tell students that a little word like *play* can become a big word when parts are added to the beginning and ending of the word. Write words that have *play* in them. Have the words pronounced, and talk about how the meaning of the word changes. Have students suggest other words with *play*. Here are some starters:

plays	played	playing	player	players
playful	playfully	playable	replay	playfulness
misplay	ballplayer	outplay	overplay	playground
playhouse	playoff	playpen	playwright	screenplay

Other roots which have many words include:

work	pieceworker	workable	homework
worked	rework	groundwork	network
working	legwork	housework	outwork
worker	unworkable	nonworker	woodwork
teamwork	overworked	paperwork	schoolwork
workers	hardworking	workshop	workout

agree	agreeable	agreeably
disagreement	agreed	agreement
nonagreement	agreeableness	agreeing
disagreeable	disagreeably	disagreeableness

create	creates	created	creature
creator	creative	creating	creatively
creativity	uncreative	creation	creations
creatures	recreation	recreational	

Sometimes, there are root words whose meaning must be taught so that students can see how words in that family are related in meaning. Here is an example for the word *port*.

Write the words *reporter, portable,* and *export* on the board. Pronounce the words as you underline the *port* in each. Tell students that many words in English have the word *port* in them. Tell them to listen as you tell them some meaning for the three words on the board to see if they can hear a meaning all the words share:

A reporter carries a story back to tell others.

Something you can carry with you is portable.

When you export something, you take or carry it out of the country.

Help students understand that *port* often means "carry or take." Next, write this list of words on the board, one at a time, and help students see how the meanings change but are still related to *port:*

```
port
export
exportable
nonexportable
import
importer
transport
transportation
```

Label this column of words "Carry or Take."

Begin another column with the words *portion* and *portrait.* Underline the *port.* Help students see that not all words which have *port* in them have a meaning related to *carry* or *take.* Tell students that when they see a word containing *port* whose meaning they do not know, they should try to figure out a meaning related to *take* or *carry* and see if that meaning makes sense in the sentence they are reading. Have students set up their paper in two columns, as your board is, and call out some words, some of which have the meaning of *carry* or *take* and some of which don't. Some possibilities are:

importer	**exporter**	**airport**
deport	**unimportant**	**porter**
portray	**passport**	**misreport**
support	**nonsupport**	**opportunity**
seaport	**important**	**portfolio**

You could do a similar activity with the root *press.* Write the words *depression, impress,* and *repress* on the board. Pronounce the words as you underline the *press* in each. Tell students that many words in English have the word *press* in them. Tell them to listen as you tell them some meanings for the words on the board to see if they can hear a meaning all the words share: "You make a *depression* when you push something down. You feel *depression* when you feel pushed down. When you *repress* a feeling, you push it out of your mind. You *impress* people when you push your good image into their minds." Help students understand that *press* often means "push."

Next, write this list of words on the board one at a time and help students see how the meanings change but are still related to *press:*

press

express

expressible

inexpressible

oppress

oppressive

oppressiveness

Tell students that when they see a word containing *press* whose meaning they do not know they should try to figure out a meaning related to push and see if that meaning makes sense in the sentence they are reading.

Begin another column with the word *cypress*. Have students notice that *cypress* ends in *press* but there does not appear to be any "push" meaning in *cypress*. Here are some words, only one of which does not have any "push" meaning relationship!

expression	**expressway**	**inexpressible**
compression	**pressure**	**pressurize**
impressive	**unimpressed**	**repressive**
suppress	**empress**	**irrepressible**
antidepressant		

Cross-Checking Big Words

Because "guessing" is often the only strategy used by children with big words, this chapter began with a caution that students should not just guess words based on a few letters. Cross-checking meaning with whatever letters, morphemes, or chunks you can use, however, is a useful strategy for figuring out big words. Two strategies that specifically teach cross-checking follow.

Using Meaning and Morphemes

These activities are similar to those described in Chapter Two for helping children use their knowledge about consonants, blends, and digraphs. In these activities, however, prefixes and suffixes will be revealed.

For each lesson, you will need to write sentences on the board or overhead transparency. Cover the word to be guessed in such a way that one or more letters can later be revealed as clues. For this lesson, cover each of the underlined words with two pieces of paper, one to cover the first syllable and one to cover the rest of the word. Write sentences such as these, with underlined words covered:

> **To stay healthy, you need <u>exercise</u>.**
>
> **This chair is very <u>uncomfortable</u>.**
>
> **The police were called out to investigate the mysterious <u>disappearance</u>.**
> **I thought I saw my friend, but when he turned around, I realized I was <u>mistaken</u>.**

Remind students that many words can be figured out by thinking about what would make sense in a sentence and seeing if the letters in the word match what one is thinking of.

Have students read the first sentence and guess what the covered word is. Next to the sentence, write each guess that makes sense. If a guess does not make sense, explain why not, but do not write this guess.

When you have written several guesses, remove the paper covering the first syllable. Erase any guesses that do not begin with this syllable and ask if there are any more guesses that "make sense in this sentence and start like this."

If there are more guesses, write these. Be sure all guesses both make sense and start correctly.

Uncover the word. See if the word you uncover is one the students guessed. If the students have the correct guess, praise their efforts. If not, say, "That was a tough one!"

You may want to do some lessons in which you cover the words with three pieces of paper, one for the prefix, one for the suffix and one to cover the rest of the word.

The Wheel

The popular game show *Wheel of Fortune* is premised on the idea that meaning and some letters allow you to figure out many words. In this game, meaning is provided by the category to which the words belong. A variation of this game can be used to introduce polysyllabic words and teach students to use meaning and all the letters they know. Here is how to play The Wheel.

Remind students that many words can be figured out, even when we can't decode all the chunks, if we think about what makes sense and whether it has the parts we do know in the right places. Ask students who have watched *Wheel of Fortune* to explain how it is played. Then explain, step by step, how your version of The Wheel will be different:

1. Contestants guess all letters without considering if they are consonants or vowels.

2. They must have all letters filled in before they can say the word. (This is to encourage them to learn to spell!)

3. They will win paper clips instead of great prizes!

4. Vanna will not be there to turn letters!

Write the category for the game on the board and draw blanks for each letter in the first word.

Have a student begin by asking, "Is there a. . . ?" If the student guesses a correct letter, fill that letter in. Give that student one paper clip for each time that letter occurs. Let the student continue to guess letters until he or she gets a "No!" When a student asks for a letter that is not there, write the letter above the puzzle and go on to the next student.

Make sure that all letters are filled in before anyone is allowed to guess. (This really shows them the importance of spelling and attending to common spelling patterns!) Give the person who correctly guesses the word five bonus paper clips. Just as in other games, if someone says the answer out of turn, immediately award the bonus paper clips to the person whose turn it was. The student having the most paper clips at the end is the winner!

Spelling Big Words

Many of the activities described in this chapter help students learn to spell big words. Of course, most students learn to spell the word-wall words. They also learn to spell as they manipulate letters to make words and as they learn about how prefixes, suffixes, and root words combine to make a variety of words. Because they have to spell the entire word to win at The Wheel, they are acutely aware of how big words are spelled.

To achieve independence in spelling big words, however, students must learn that because there is not just one way to spell many English spelling patterns, you need both a good sense of the probable spelling and a visual memory for the word. Lacking a clear visual memory for the word, you should come up with the most probable spelling and then check the dictionary. Lessons similar to those described in Chapter Two can be used to help students learn how to "look it up when you can't spell it!" But, here is an example for words that end in *-able* and *-ible:*

Write the words *miserable* and *enjoyable* in a column on the board. Have students notice that both words end in *-able,* and point out that sometimes words with that ending mean "able to be something": "When something is enjoyable, you are able to enjoy it." Label this column *-able.*

You may want to do a similar lesson with words that end in *-el, -le,* and *-al:*

freckle	circle	model	general
practical	cradle	cable	physical
label	medal	apple	terrible
pretzel	motel	cereal	tropical

Other chunks whose spelling must be checked are *-tion* and *-sion:*

solution	caution	decision	extension
temptation	position	confusion	construction
conclusion	motion	pension	conversation

Linking Spelling and Meaning

In addition to helping readers figure out the pronunciation of big words, an understanding of morphemic relationships can help children make sense of a seemingly chaotic spelling system. Here are some of the anomalies of our English spelling system which make many children think there is no system!

Why does *bomb* have a *b* at the end and *sign* have a seemingly worthless *g*?

Why is there a *c* in *muscle*?

Why is the second syllable of *composition* spelled with an *o* while a syllable that sounds the same in *competition* is spelled with an *e*?

To help children understand that "there is method in this seeming madness," send them into the dictionary to find other words with the same root. When they find words such as *bombard* and *bombastic*, the *b* at the end of *bomb* will make sense. *Signal, signature,* and other related words will explain the *g* in *sign* and *muscular* will explain the *c* in *muscle*. Finding the *compose/composition* and *compete/competition* relationship will help students understand why the second syllable of *composition* and *competition* sound alike but are spelled differently.

The spelling patterns exemplified by these words are the kinds of patterns that exist between morphemically related words. Templeton (1991) put it most succinctly when he said students need to learn that "words that are related in meaning are often related in spelling as well, despite changes in sound" (p. 194). Teachers should take every opportunity to point out this relationship when words are being introduced and when working with children in editing their writing for public display. Children should learn a mental strategy that goes something like this:

When you are not sure how to spell a big word, try to think of a related word.

Many examples of these meaning-spelling links and some sample activities for them can be found in *Words Their Way* (Bear, Invernizzi, and Templeton, 1995).

Assessing Children's Developing Word Knowledge

One of the most exciting and promising signs of progress in elementary classrooms today is to watch teachers develop and use assessment measures which actually reflect what different children know and can do and how they are growing. In many classrooms, tests and graded worksheets are being replaced with anecdotal records and portfolios which are more valid, reliable, and authentic measures of children's success. Teachers are using running records (Clay, 1994) and tape-recorded readings and retellings to determine children's growth in reading. In North Carolina, for example, the state guidelines now list actual books that children should be able to read fluently with comprehension at each grade level. Writing samples are collected periodically and evaluated to determine how children are growing in their writing ability. Because reading and writing fluency and enjoyment are the two major goals of literacy instruction, running records and samples of children's reading and writing should be the major vehicles for assessing literacy growth.

In observing children's reading, teachers can look at the errors or miscues that children make and determine what word-identification strategies they are using. Good readers will self-correct many of their miscues. This usually indicates that they are using context to check that what they are reading makes sense. Successful self-correction is an excellent indicator that the reader is using all three cueing systems—meaning (semantic), sounding like language (syntactic), and letter-sound knowledge (graphophonic)—successfully. Other students tend to overuse context—their miscues make sense but don't have most of the letter-sound relationships of the original word. Finally, there are students who overuse letter-sound knowledge. Their miscues look and sound a lot like the original words but they don't make any sense. By observing children's reading, we can determine what strategies they are using and what kind of instructional activities we might provide for them.

Writing samples also show growth in word knowledge. In addition to writings on self-selected topics, many schools are now collecting focused writing samples two or three times a year and looking at these to determine growth in writing ability and word knowledge. A focused writing sample collected for assessment purposes should have a topic specified about which most children have good general knowledge, and children should write on this topic with no assistance from the teacher or any other child. Some examples of topics used in primary classrooms include:

My Favorite Things To Do

What I Like to Do at School

An Animal I Would Like to Have for a Pet

Many schools have the child write about the same topic at several different points in time—May of kindergarten, January and May of first grade, January and May of second grade, for example. These topic-focused, nonassisted first drafts are then compared to determine an individual child's writing growth. In addition to a slew of valuable information about how the child writes—sentence sense, topic sense, word choice, writing conventions, etc.—these samples yield valuable information about the child's developing word knowledge. To look at the child's word knowledge, teachers consider how words are represented, including such things as:

Uses pictures and letters that can be read only by the writer.

Uses initial and final letters to spell words, sometimes with a random vowel thrown in (*bt* or *bet* for *bat*).

Spells some words conventionally.

Uses letter-sound spellings which are phonetically correct and can be read by others (*benz* for *beans*; *lat* for *late*).

Uses spelling patterns but not necessarily the correct one (*beens* for *beans*, *lait* for *late*).

Spells most high-frequency words (word-wall words) conventionally.

Puts endings on words but does not use spelling changes (*bigest*; *comeing*).

Makes needed spelling changes when adding endings (*biggest*; *coming*).

Generally chooses correct spelling pattern (*beans*, *late*).

Spells big words using one-syllable word knowledge (*vacashun* for *vacation*; *delishus* for *delicious*; *wonderfull* for *wonderful*).

Shows knowledge of special big-word patterns when spelling big words (*vacation*, *delicious*, *wonderful*).

Running records and tape-recorded readings along with self-selected topic writing and focused writing samples provide the most authentic, valid, and reliable measures of each child's developing word knowledge. There are two tests, however, which along with the real reading and writing measures, will give teachers additional information about children's word knowledge.

Gentry and Gillet (1993) suggest that teachers of young children use both writing samples and a Developmental Spelling Test to determine the developmental spelling level of children and to verify growth in their spelling abilities. They observe that looking at writing samples gives us a great deal of information but may not tell the whole story. Some children use many words in their writing which are way beyond what a child at their level could be expected to spell. Their writing might contain many more phonetic and transitional spellings than the writing of children whose writing uses words closer to grade-level expectations. Other children restrict themselves to words they can spell or whose correct spelling they can find in the room, by asking another child, or by looking for the word in books. Looking at the writing samples of these children would lead us to believe they were conventional spellers when their actual spelling ability might be inflated by their proclivity to spell it right!

The Developmental Spelling Test consists of ten words which are dictated to children and then analyzed to determine the level of their spelling and word knowledge. Other words could be used, but the words Gentry and Gillet suggest are:

monster
united
dress
bottom
hiked
human
eagle
closed
bumped
type

Once children have spelled these words as best they can, Gentry and Gillet suggest analyzing their spelling using the following stages:

The Precommunicative Stage: Children in kindergarten through second grade move through stages as they use letters to represent words in writing. Their first attempts at writing are collections of scribbles, circles, and lines with a few letters thrown in at random. These letters usually are just there, and any connection between these letters and the words they are thinking is pure coincidence. This stage of writing is often referred to as scribbling.

The Semiphonetic Stage: The second stage can be seen when words begin to be represented by a letter or two. The word *monster* may be written with just an *m* or an *mr* or a *mtr*. *Type* might be written with just a *t* or *tp*. This stage indicates that the child is beginning to understand letter-sound relationships and knows the consonant letters which represent some sounds.

The Phonetic Stage: In the third stage, vowels appear—not necessarily always the right vowels, but vowels, are used and most sounds are represented by at least one letter. Phonetic spelling of *monster* might include *munstr* and *mostr*. *Type* will probably be spelled *tip*. You can usually tell when a child is in the phonetic stage because you can read most of what children in this stage write.

The Transitional Stage: In this stage all sounds are represented and the spelling is usually a possible English spelling, just not the correct spelling. *Monster* in this stage might be spelled *monstir* or *monstur*. *Type* is probably spelled *tipe*.

The Conventional Stage: Finally, the child reaches the stage of conventional spelling in which most words which a child at that grade level could be expected to spell correctly.

The Developmental Spelling Test is a valuable assessment tool. For samples, specific scoring information and a variety of practical spelling suggestions, I highly recommend Gentry and Gillet's book *Teaching Kids to Spell*.

A final possibility to consider when assessing children's word knowledge is The Names Test. I developed The Names Test (Cunningham, 1990) several years ago when working with a group of older remedial readers. These boys were good context users, and it was quite difficult to determine what they knew about letter-sound patterns when they were reading contextually because they were such good context users. I wanted a measure of their word identification ability that was not confounded by context but which was not just a list of words. Reading a list of words is a rather "unnatural act," and choosing the words is quite difficult. If you choose words most children have in their listening vocabularies, you run the risk of also choosing words they know as sight words and thus don't have to decode, and you could overestimate their letter-sound knowledge. If you choose very obscure words, they probably don't have them in their listening vocabularies and thus can't use the "sounds right" clue to check their probable pronunciation. Nonsense words have the same problems. Nothing we ask kids to do is more unnatural than reading a list of made-up words (well, almost nothing!) and many children try to make the nonsense word into a word they have heard of; the nonsense-word test would thus be an underestimate of their decoding ability.

There is one type of word, however, which children hear often—and thus have in their listening vocabularies—but which they don't read often—and thus are not apt to have already learned them as sight words. Names are heard all over the place. Names are a big part of every TV and radio program, and usually these names are pronounced but not read. Names are one type of word that most children have a lot more of in their listening vocabularies than in their sight vocabularies; thus, I used names for the source of words to measure decoding ability not confounded by context. In addition to their more-often-heard-than-read quality, names have another advantage for a word-reading test. We do sometimes read lists of names. Teachers and others often "call the role," thus reading a list is a somewhat more natural real-reading task than most other word-list reading tasks. Here is the Names Test with directions and suggestions for analyzing children's responses.

Procedures for Administering and Scoring the Names Test (Cunningham, 1990)

Preparing the Instrument

1. Type or print the 35 names on a sheet of paper or card stock. Make sure the print size is appropriate for the age of the students being tested.
2. For students who might perceive reading an entire list of names as being too formidable, type or print the names on index cards, so they can be read individually.
3. Prepare a protocol (scoring) sheet. Do this by typing the list of names in a column and following each name with a blank line to be used for recording a student's responses.

Administering the Names Test

1. Administer the Names Test individually in a quiet, distraction-free location.
2. Explain to the student that she or he is to pretend to be a teacher who must read a list of names of students in the class. Direct the student to read the names as if taking attendance.
3. Have the student read the entire list. Inform the student that you will not be able to help with difficult names, and encourage him or her to "make a guess if you are not sure."
4. Write a check on the protocol sheet for each name read correctly. Write phonetic spellings for names that are mispronounced.

Scoring and Interpreting the Names Test

1. Count a word correct if all syllables are pronounced correctly regardless of where the student places the accent. For example, either Yó/lan/da or Yo/lán/da would be acceptable.
2. For words in which the vowel pronunciation depends on which syllable the consonant is placed with, count them correct for either pronunciation. For example, either Ho/mer or Hom/er would be acceptable.
3. Count the number of names read correctly, and analyze those mispronounced, looking for patterns indicative of decoding strengths and weaknesses.

The Names Test of Decoding
by Patricia M. Cunningham
(with additional names by F. A. Dufflemeyer)

Jay Conway	Chuck Hoke
Kimberly Blake	Homer Preston
Cindy Sampson	Ginger Yale
Stanley Shaw	Glen Spencer
Flo Thornton	Grace Brewster
Ron Smitherman	Vance Middleton
Bernard Pendergraph	Floyd Sheldon
Austin Shepherd	Neal Wade
Joan Brooks	Thelma Rinehart
Tim Cornell	Yolanda Clark
Roberta Slade	Gus Quincy
Chester Wright	Patrick Tweed
Wendy Swain	Fred Sherwood
Dee Skidmore	Ned Westmoreland
Troy Whitlock	Zane Anderson
Shane Fletcher	Dean Bateman
Bertha Dale	Jake Murphy
Gene Loomis	

References

Bear, D. B., Invernizzi, M., and Templeton, S. (1995) *Words Their Way: A Developmental Approach to Phonics, Spelling and Vocabulary, K-8*. New York: Macmillan/Merrill.

Canney, G., and Schreiner, R. (1977). "A Study of the Effectiveness of Selected Syllabication Rules and Phonogram Patterns for Word Attack." *Reading Research Quarterly, 12*, 102–124.

Clay, M. M. (1994). *Reading Recovery: A Guidebook for Teachers in Training*. Portsmouth, NH: Heinemann.

Cunningham, P. M. (1990). "The Names Test: A Quick Assessment of Decoding Ability." *The Reading Teacher, 44*, 124–129.

Cunningham, P. M. (1978). "Decoding Polysyllabic Words: An Alternative Strategy." *Journal of Reading, 21,* 608–614.

Cunningham, P. M., and Hall, D. P. (1994). *Making Big Words*. Good Apple.

Gentry, J. R., and Gillet, J. W. (1993). *Teaching Kids to Spell*. Portsmouth, NH: Heinemann.

Templeton, S. (1991). Teaching and Learning the English Spelling System: Reconceptualizing Method and Purpose. *The Elementary School Journal, 92*, 185–201.

Tough Questions and
Not Simple Answers

Real teachers ask tough questions! There are no simple answers to these complex issues, but I will share some of my thoughts on them.

This all sounds fine, but when do you find the time to do all this?

Time is the most precious commodity any teacher has, and like money, there is never enough of it! For that reason, you must set priorities, and your activities must be planned to accomplish two things at once, at the very least. You also must decide how much time an activity is worth and stick to the time limits you set for yourself. Many teachers find that it helps to do certain things at the same time each day. The children then expect to do it and get in the habit of being ready. One teacher calls out her word-wall words as a settling down activity right after the morning break. The children know that when the timer rings at 10:20, they should take a piece of scratch paper and number it from one to five because at 10:21, the teacher begins to call out words from the word wall. In this classroom, the words are called out, written, chanted, and checked by 10:30 sharp, every morning.

Many of the activities in this book are "filler" or "sponge" activities. You can do a quick game of The Wheel or Mystery Word Match in two minutes if you have handy, somewhere, the words and clues you want to use. You can place on the board each morning one or two sentences for cross-checking, which you do whenever there are a few extra minutes. This makes for especially efficient use of time because students spend a lot of individual time during the day reading the sentences and thinking about what the covered-up words might be. They even talk to one another about their guesses. By the time you get ready, they have lots of ideas and are eager for you to reveal some letters so that they can figure out the covered-up words that have been teasing them all day.

Setting priorities and time limits is easy, but sticking to the time limits is almost impossible.

That's why you need a timer! I can't imagine that teachers are not all issued a new one each year along with the chalk and the gradebook! Setting a timer for the amount of time you want to spend on an activity keeps you and the students moving along at the brisk pace essential for optimal learning. Activities, such as making words, cross-checking, and decoding new words by comparing them to known word families should be scheduled for 20 minutes, maximum. They should end before everyone wants them to end. The timer should sound and the children should say, "Can't we do just one more?" The teacher, depending on the day and her mood, may respond, "Sorry, the timer just went off," or, "O.K. but this is the last one because we have used all our time." Timers force us to decide how much time an activity is worth and then help us stick to our decision.

I know that I as the teacher use my time well, but sometimes I feel that student time is not always well used.

That's true and I have purposely included here many activities that require minimal teaching time but maximize student thinking time. Once you have a "Big Word of the Day" board started for which each student can nominate a word each day and the box and ballots set up for students to write their nominations on, you have to spend only a few minutes at the end of each day reading the nominees and letting students vote for the best big word. Teachers who model how they figured out a big word and then give every student an index card and the homework assignment to find a big word and write it on the card are using very little teaching time and maximizing student thinking time.

Another way to maximize student time-on-task is to use a variety of every-pupil response activities. Every pupil is responding when each student writes and chants the spelling of the word-wall words or makes a chart like the teacher's chart and writes the new word under the word it rhymes with or manipulates the letters to make words called out by the teacher. As a general rule, if children's bodies are not doing anything externally, their minds are not doing anything internally.

What did you mean when you said teachers had to be doing at least two things at once?

I meant, you have to integrate—both among the language arts and content-area subjects. Activities in this book are designed to teach both decoding and spelling. There are almost no good spellers who cannot decode words. Separating spelling from phonics instruction seems both wasteful of time and less than effective in terms of how children learn about our alphabetic system. Similarly, reading and writing support one another and teaching them together makes the best use of time and provides students with less "choppy" learning experiences.

Many of the words that students need to learn to spell and that offer real-world opportunities for applying their decoding skills occur as students read and write in science and social studies. This is true for all words, but is particularly true for big words. When you select words from content areas and use them in spelling and decoding activities, you "kill two birds with one stone."

What should I do with my phonics masters?

Burn them!

You don't really mean that. Don't they need to practice their skills?

Actually, I am sure there could be some useful phonics activities students could practice independently with a photocopied sheet. (In fact, I must confess that I helped produce some phonics workbooks once and tried to make them as "application level" and "activity oriented" as possible!) Unfortunately, the possible good use of phonics masters is so overwhelmingly outweighed by the current enormous waste of teacher time, student time, and paper that I have to say we would be better off burning them and seeing what we could do without them!

Yes, students do need practice, but not the type of passive practice provided by circling words or filling in letters. The quote with which this book began, "They know the skills; they just don't use them," may be explained in large part by the incredible omnipresence of phonics masters. Children learn what they are taught, and consequently they can fill in, circle, and match just about any sound. What they can't do is figure out a new word with those very same sounds!

Students need active practice manipulating letters and sounds, looking at words for patterns and learning to expect some predictability in our sound system. Most important, they need to spend their independent work time reading and writing so they can apply what they know where it really matters, to the words they need to read and write.

Well, I, for one, would love to burn them, but then what about the tests?

Now, that's what we truly need to burn! Seriously, there is no way to test anyone's ability to *apply* what they know about letters and sounds except to observe whether they use this knowledge in actual reading and writing. The tests, which measure isolated bits of knowledge and not whether this knowledge is or can ever be used, are miseducative and should no longer be imposed on teachers or children!

But, how will we know which children are learning phonics? Don't we need assessment?

Yes, we do need assessment; but the assessment must, in this case, take the form of observation. Children's ability to figure out an unknown word should be observed when they are reading and encountering new words. Children's ability to master our spelling system is best assessed by keeping portfolios of writing samples. Teachers who work with children on a daily basis have opportunities to observe how children are responding during the activities and what they actually do while reading and writing. Many teachers designate a fifth of their children as Monday children; a fifth, Tuesday; a fifth, Wednesday; and so forth. Each day, the teacher makes some anecdotal notes about the reading and writing strengths and weaknesses of the designated children. These records give the teacher real information about what the children can do and what additional instruction they may need. There are some additional assessment suggestions at the end of Chapter One and Chapter Four.

I teach second grade and my children are "all over the place" in their decoding and spelling ability. What can I do?

The natural diversity of children is what makes teaching such a trick! All children are not alike. They learn things at different rates and in different ways and have various strengths and weaknesses. No one can meet the needs of all the children all the time. But, we must meet the needs of every child at some time during the day.

In general, the more "real" the activity, the closer we come to meeting the needs of all the children. Children who select books to read usually choose books they can read, and develop their reading abilities more quickly because they care about what they are reading. Writing has no level. Children write at all different levels and, with support and encouragement, they become better writers.

As teaching activities become more removed from reading and writing, the differences in children's abilities present instructional problems. One of the principles in this book is that, as much as possible, activities should have different levels of difficulty and should allow children with different abilities to get something out of the activity. Take the word-wall activities, for example. In most second-grade classrooms, most of the children can already read most words we add to the word wall. Their daily word-wall practice helps them learn to spell these highly frequent words. But, in every class, there are a few children who could already spell a lot of these words. Is it a waste of their time to write and chant the spelling of these words? Most teachers who have used a word-wall would tell you that the few children who can already spell most of these words at the beginning of second grade are not yet automatic with the spelling. As they are writing, they have to "stop and think" about how to spell *who* or about which *to* (t-o, t-w-o, or t-o-o) belongs in their sentence. Teachers believe that the word-wall activity is not a waste of time for these children because the daily writing and chanting moves them to an adultlike level of automaticity in spelling these highly frequent words.

There are, of course, second graders who are not yet able to read many of the words we add to the word wall. These children take longer to learn to spell the words, but through the daily writing and chanting, they learn to read them and to find them when they need them in their writing. Word-wall activities in most classrooms have "something for everyone," but that something is different for different children!

Most of the activities in this book were designed to have "something for everyone." They begin with an easy "warm-up" and end with something to challenge your stars. I call there multilevel activities. You may, however, want to select some activities which only a few of your children need and pull those children together for that activity. Sometimes, you can get an adult or older child tutor who can do some of these activities with just the children who need them. Pairing your children for some cooperative ventures may also be a way of meeting the needs of the many different children you teach.

I teach middle school remedial readers and my kids can't decode or spell. But, isn't it too late for them?

We have successfully used most of these activities, and particularly the activities in Chapters Three and Four, with middle school students. Often, there is a lot of resistance on their part to anything that even vaguely resembles the phonics they failed at for so many years. We are particularly careful with remedial students to avoid all jargon and rules, and we try to use game-like formats whenever possible. They particularly like Making Big Words, described in Chapter Four. They also enjoy the games, such as Mystery Word Match and The Wheel. We use word walls with them to try to give them some big words they can read and spell, and we choose highly potent words such as *championship, athletics, gymnasium,* and *competition.*

The single most important thing, however, with older remedial students is to get them reading and writing. We gather the widest range of easy-to-read, teen-interest materials and make both daily reading and sharing and daily writing and sharing a priority. Decoding and spelling activities take a well-deserved back seat to these two real literacy events.

Many of these activities would be good in science or social studies, but my school is departmentalized, so I have only one hour each day for reading and language arts. How can I make this work for me?

Unfortunately, your inability to integrate means that time is not as well used, and children must get a greater sense of fragmentation in what they are learning. Perhaps you could share this book with the people responsible for the departmentalization and at least bring this important decision up for reconsideration. If not, you just have to do what you can. At least you can integrate reading and writing and do the activities your students need and that are least content oriented. You might also share some of the activities you wish you could do with a friendly science or social studies teacher.

Aren't there some children who just can't ever learn sounds?

There may be. There are certainly some children who can't learn to decode and spell the way we have traditionally taught it. In synthetic phonics programs, where children begin by learning the sounds in isolation and then blend them into words, we have children who cannot remember the sounds and others who, once they have made the individual sounds, cannot blend them to a word they know. In analytic programs, we have children who learn the jargon and rules but never learn to apply this to figuring out unknown words.

While I'm not sure there are children who can't learn sounds, I am absolutely sure that any "one-way" approach to sounds will result in some children not being able to learn. If you look through the activities in this book, you see much variety in the mode of presentation and the thinking required to participate in the activities. Every teacher will have favorite activities, but because children learn in so many different ways, the most successful teachers do many different activities to teach each important strategy. All activities in this book have been successfully done by some teachers with some children. To meet the needs of all your children, begin with those activities your children need and that just naturally appeal to you. As you meet success with these activities, branch out to some with which you are not as immediately comfortable. Then, vary the daily activities so that across the week, your decoding and spelling program has the essential repetition with the equally essential variety!

The Theory and the Research—The Why Underlying the How

Each year, at the National Reading Conference (NRC) annual meeting, one of its members reviews the research in an area considered of critical interest to the field of reading. In 1991, phonics was the hot topic and I was chosen to review the research. Here is an adapted/updated version of the talk I gave. It (Cunningham, 1992) contains the research and theoretical base for the instructional activities in *Phonics They Use*.

What Kind of Phonics Instruction Will We Have?*
Patricia M. Cunningham
Wake Forest University
National Reading Conference, Palm Springs, December 1991

The question of instruction in phonics has aroused a lot of controversy. Some educators have held to the proposition that phonetic training is not only futile and wasteful but also harmful to the best interests of a reading program. Others believe that since the child must have some means of attacking strange words, instruction in phonics is imperative. There have been disputes also relative to the amount of phonics to be taught, the time when the teaching should take place and the methods to be used. In fact, the writer knows of no problem around which more disputes have centered.
Paul McKee—1934 (p. 191)

Clearly, the phonics question has been plaguing the field of reading for a long time. In this review, I will try to (1) convince you that we are always going to have some phonics instruction and that WE have a responsibility to influence the form that instruction takes, (2) share with you my own struggles as a teacher and a researcher with the phonics dilemma, (3) review the major research findings of the past 20 years, and (4) describe phonics instruction which appears to be consistent with that research.

There Will be Some Phonics Instruction

Many reading experts today are opposed to any kind of phonics instruction. Some believe that decoding plays no role in meaningful reading. Others accept the notion that readers use letter-sound knowledge to decode unfamiliar words, but believe that readers will discover whatever they need to know. There is a fairly pervasive attitude which seems to translate: "Phonics

*From P. M. Cunningham (1992). "What kind of phonics instruction will we have?" In C. K. Kinzer and D. J. Leu (eds.), *Literacy Research, Theory, and Practice: Views from Many Perspectives*, Forty-first Yearbook of the National Reading Conference, pp. 17–31. Chicago: National Reading Conference.

happens but you can't teach it!" The reality is that teachers do teach it and parents demand that it be taught. In the week prior to NRC, as I was trying to figure out how to convince the NRC audience that there would always be some kind of phonics being taught, three persuasive events occurred.

A long article with photographs of mostly minority children headlined "Opposed to Whole Language, Houston Schools Revert to Phonics" appeared in the November 20, 1992, *Education Week*.

> **Disenchanted with or opposed to whole-language approaches to teaching reading, educators at eight Houston elementary schools have persuaded local school officials to allow them to return to a traditional phonics-based reading instruction program this year. Teachers and principals at the schools argued that their students, many of whom are from low-income families were doing poorly under the whole-language method, at least in part because the students' parents were not providing the at-home support needed to make the whole-language approach work. . . .**

The article goes on to explain that these schools are being given $70,000 to go back to DISTAR, "a program which is heavily structured and paces children through repetition sound drills and was dropped because its results did not meet expectations." The teachers in these Houston schools clearly thought that whole language or phonics was an either/or proposition, and after trying the DISTAR approach to phonics and getting less than satisfactory results, they had tried "whole language" and were now dropping that and reverting to DISTAR.

In the same week, this item appeared on the front page of the *Greensboro News & Record Sunday* paper:

> **Mike looks at the work sheet and bears down on the five-letter word he's been asked to read. "It's got an E at the end," he tells himself, "so it must be a long I." Then he begins "sounding out" the word, letter-by-letter. "Sss. Sp. Spike?"**
>
> **"Yes," reassures his tutor.**
>
> **Mike moves down the list of words built around the letter I, the vowel he has tackled since starting the private tutoring lessons in August. . . . Mike reads the words carefully. *Slide. Limp. Flirt. Flip. Rip. Bird.***
>
> **"You couldn't have done that three weeks ago," his tutor tells him.**

The article goes on to explain that Mike asked for a tutor to teach him to read three months after graduating from Guilford County's Northeast High School. Mike's inability to read is attributed to his lack of phonics, and this grueling three-week-long letter-by-letter sounding of lists of words containing the vowel I is what the public is led to think Mike should have gotten a long time ago!

The final item which caught my attention occurred on Sunday night. My teenage son likes oldies, and on Sunday nights, he listens to "Cousin Brucie" on the radio. Every 15 minutes or so, the oldies are interrupted by an ad for *Hooked on Phonics*. This ad explains that there are only 44 sounds in the English language and that for $149.00, you can order a set of tapes which will teach anyone "from four to forty-four" to read. It is clear from the continuing nationwide advertising blitz that a lot of people are sending in their money to get the tapes and books with the lists of phonetically controlled words.

The kind of phonics instruction exemplified by these three examples is the worst kind of phonics. It is devoid of meaning and isolated from real reading and writing. Furthermore, the letter-by-letter sounding it teaches is not consistent with what we know about how phonics actually works. This kind of phonics instruction is selling, however, because teachers and parents know that phonics is useful, that all good readers can decode words, and that most poor readers can't and because it is what is for sale. It is not, however, the kind of phonics instruction we should have.

My Own Phonics Struggle

My fate was probably sealed in 1949 when I was a first grader at High Street School in Westerly, Rhode Island. In the morning, we were divided into reading groups and read about the adventures of Sally, Dick, Jane, Puff, and Spot. After lunch each day, we all pulled out bright blue phonics books and sounded out words. Little did I know that at five years old, I was thrust right into the middle of the sight word/phonics controversy.

The year 1965 found me teaching first grade in Key West, Florida. I taught the phonics in my basal manual, and most children learned to distinguish short vowels from long vowels. The children in my top group even developed the ability to "sound out" new words, although even then I didn't quite believe that what they did when they came to a new word was, in any way, related to what I was teaching them about phonics. One day, I overheard a boy remark to a friend, "The short vowels are pretty short but the long ones look pretty short, too." His friend then proceeded to explain it to him. "It's simple. The little ones are the short ones and the capital ones are the long ones!" Although I continued to teach first grade and the vowel rules for several years, my faith in them was badly shaken!

I got my master's degree in Reading from Florida State in 1968. "Linguistics" was the buzzword at that time, and I thought that "linguistic readers" were going to solve the decoding problems of our poor readers. I got a chance to try this out with a whole class full of fourth-grade poor readers. Armed with the Merrill Linguistic Readers and the SRA Basic Reading Series, I abandoned phonics rules for linguistic patterns. Things went pretty well for the first month. The students learned all the short *a* patterns and read about Dan in his tan van. As we moved on, however, they began to confuse the previously learned patterns with the new ones. Worse yet, I realized that the children had stopped trying to make sense of what they were reading and were simply sounding out the patterns!

By 1970, context was the only remaining tool in my decoding arsenal. "Say 'blank' and read the rest of the sentence and then go back and think about what would make sense," was my 1970 brand of decoding instruction.

In 1971, I found myself in Terre Haute, Indiana, as the special reading teacher at the Indiana State University Laboratory School. All day, I worked with poor readers. Mostly, I tried to get these students to enjoy reading and to talk about what they read. I did almost no phonics instruction, but it did worry me that almost all the poor readers had little ability to decode an unfamiliar word. My "real challenges" arrived after lunch each day. Rod and Erin were sixth graders of normal intelligence who had been in remedial reading since second grade and who read at the second-grade level. Both boys were fluent with all the most-commonly occurring words and were excellent users of picture and context clues. They could understand anything they could read and most of what you read to them. They had been scheduled for 45 minutes alone with me each day because they were to go on the junior high next year and their parents were very worried that, after all these years, they still hadn't "caught on to reading."

For both Rod and Erin, the problem was clear-cut. They knew what reading was and that you were to make meaning from it. They enjoyed being read to and even enjoyed reading the high-interest, low-vocabulary books I could find that they could read themselves. They simply had not learned to decode! For the first semester, I taught Rod and Erin "word families." They were very competitive and I made Go Fish and Old Maid and Concentration games, which they could win by matching and saying rhyming words. We also made charts of rhyming words and wrote jingles and riddles, which were awful but which appealed to their sixth-grade silliness.

In addition to rhyming games and writing rhymes, each day we read together and I reminded them of the one strategy I had taught them. Both boys knew that when you came to a short word you didn't know, you should look to see if it would rhyme with a word you did know. When they couldn't think of a rhyming word, I prompted them with one. They used this strategy when they were reading and were amazed to discover that they could figure out even unusual names—*Tran, Zep, Kurt.*

Unfortunately, their newfound decoding ability did not transfer to bigger words. I taught them a few simple syllable-division rules and they could sometimes figure out a two-syllable word, the syllables of which were familiar rhyming patterns—*zinger*, *target*, *pastor*. If a word had more than six letters, however, they couldn't even begin to do anything with it and would just skip it and go on!

By March, the boys were reading at a strong third-grade level—sometimes fourth—if they knew a lot about the topic. I knew that their inability and unwillingness to decode long words was the remaining hurdle, but I didn't know how to teach them to figure them out. I taught them some prefixes and suffixes, but this didn't seem to help with very many words. I would drive home in the afternoons and see a big word on a billboard and ask myself, "How did I figure out that word?" I knew that I had not applied syllabication rules and then sounded out each syllable, but I didn't know what I had done.

We were at six weeks before the end of sixth grade and Rod and Erin had begun the countdown to summer and junior high! In desperation, I searched the Education Index for "polysyllabic word instruction." I didn't find much, and discounted most of what I did find. Context was what Rod and Erin were currently using. Syllabication rules weren't working (and research confirmed that!). They had learned most of the common prefixes and suffixes and that wasn't taking them very far. Finally, one article suggested teaching students to use the dictionary respelling key. "Well, that's something I haven't tried," I thought. "But, no one is ever going to stop reading and find the word in the dictionary and use the respelling key," I argued with myself.

But I decided to do it. What did I have to lose? We had to do something useful for the last six weeks, and at least they would know how to use the respelling key to pronounce a word if they would take the time to do it. For two weeks, I taught them how to use the key to figure out the pronunciation of unknown words. Then, when they understood how to do it, I gave them each a different list of five "really long" words (*conscientious*, *filibuster*, *mannequin*, *Phoenician*, *sporadically*) each day. Before we could go on to do anything interesting, they each had to find their words and use the key to figure them out and pronounce them for me!

They hated it but "it was good for them," and I was determined that they would have a big-word tool to take with them to junior high, so each day, they came in and picked up their list and their dictionaries and went to work. Ten days before the end of school, Rod walked in and picked up his list of five "humongous" words and his dictionary. He began to look up the first word, then he stopped, looked at the word and then at me. "What if I already know this word? Do I still have to look it up?" he asked.

"Well no," I responded. "I'm trying to give you a tool so that you can always pronounce any big word you ever come to, but if you know the word, you don't need the respelling key, do you?" Rod looked again at the first word, studying the letters. He then correctly pronounced: "spontaneous!" "That's right!" I exclaimed. "Now, you only have four to look up!" "Not if I know some of the others," Rod asserted. He was able to pronounce two of the other four words and only had to look up and use the key for two of the five big words. Meanwhile, Erin was studying his five words and he managed to pronounce two of his, only having to look up three.

I was astonished! "Where had they learned those words?" I wondered. For the remaining nine days of school, Rod and Erin competed to see how many words they could figure out and not have to look up. To my amazement, by the last day of school they had gotten quite good at figuring out words of four or more syllables. The respelling key, which I had taught them to use as a tool had taught them a system for independently figuring out big words. At the time I didn't understand how this miracle had occurred, but I sent Rod and Erin off to junior high more confident of their success than I had ever thought I would.

In 1972, I arrived at the University of Georgia to work on my doctorate in reading. I took my first seminar, and Dr. Ira Aaron led us to do some initial thinking about a dissertation topic. I already knew what I wanted to find out: "How do we decode an unknown word, and particularly an unknown big word?" After much reading, thinking, and discussions with other doctoral students and Dr. George Mason, my advisor, I became convinced that decoding took place in what I called a compare/contrast way. Later this would be called "decoding by analogy." In addition to my dissertation (Cunningham, 1975–76), I did quite a bit of research into analogic decoding (Cunningham, 1979; 1980; Cunningham and Guthrie, 1982; Gaskins, Downer, Anderson, Cunningham, Gaskins, Schommer, and the Teachers of the Benchmark School, 1988) which confirmed for me that decoding was neither a letter-by-letter sounding process nor a rule-based, jargon-filled process. My observations of the children I had taught as well as the research

I carried out convinced me that when readers come to unfamiliar words, they do a fast search through their cognitive word stores for similar words with the same letters in the same places. They then use these analogs to come up with a possible pronunciation which they try out and cross-check with meaning.

I understood finally that when I complained that my first graders knew the rules but didn't use them, I was right! The rules describe the system. The brain, however, is not a rule applier but a pattern detector. I also understood why teaching children linguistic patterns or "word families" was a powerful strategy if you could get them to use these spelling patterns to write and read words in meaningful texts.

By 1982, ten years after Rod and Erin had learned to read, I had figured out how they did it. Combining word-family instruction with reading and writing in which they were encouraged to use rhyming words to figure out how to pronounce or spell unknown words taught them to look for patterns in words and, most importantly that there were patterns to be found when they looked. Looking up big words in the dictionary respelling key forced them to look carefully at all the letters in the words (so that they could find them in the dictionary) and the analogs contained in the respelling key convinced them that there were patterns to be found in big words, too!

By the time I answered, to my own satisfaction, the question of how decoding happens, nobody cared! In the early eighties, schools were still using criterion-referenced testing systems which broke decoding down into multiple rules/skills. When I tried to convince teachers, publishers, and others that these rules/skills might describe the system but that they were not what you *did* when you came to an unknown word, the response was, "But the rules/skills are what is tested!" The next wave to sweep the schools was "whole language" and then nobody really cared!

In 1989, two events occurred which reignited my interest in the role of decoding in beginning reading instruction. I reviewed a prepublication copy of Marilyn Jager Adam's (1990) *Beginning to Read: Thinking and Learning about Print* and, while in the middle of reading this, I watched a Reading Recovery lesson. From reading the Adams book, I realized that there had been, mostly in the field of psychology, a huge amount of research and that we knew a lot more know about how the brain functioned in identifying words. From watching the Reading Recovery lesson, I realized that the varied activities within the 30-minute lesson represented instruction compatible with what we now knew about the reading process.

What We Have Learned in the Past 20 Years

It has been 20 years since Rod and Erin propelled me off to get a doctorate in reading. In this section I shall summarize the research that had not been done yet that would have made my teaching much less of a trial-and-error process. *Beginning to Read* (Adams, 1990) is still the best overall source for this information, but there are other important sources listed with each of the major findings.

WHAT WE KNOW ABOUT HOW GOOD READERS READ WORDS

We know a great deal more about how word recognition occurs than can be explained in this section. The theory that explains the incredibly fast ability of the brain to recognize words and associate them with meaning is called parallel distributed processing. This theory is complex but its most important tenets are easily understood. Information about a word is gained from its spelling (orthography), its pronunciation (phonology), its meaning (semantics), and the context in which the word occurs. The brain processes these sources of information in parallel, or simultaneously. The brain functions in word recognition, as it does in all other areas, as a pattern detector. Discussion of parallel distributed processing and its implications for word identification can be found in Seidenberg and McClelland, 1989; McClelland and Rumelhart, 1986; and Rumelhart and McClelland, 1986. The theory is translated and explained simply and elegantly in Adams (1990). Beyond the fact that the brain responds to many sources of information in parallel and that it functions as a pattern detector, the following specific facts seem particularly pertinent to the question of what kind of phonics instruction we should have.

Readers look at virtually all of the words and almost all the letters in those words (Rayner and Pollatsek, 1989; McConkie, Kerr, Reddix, and Zola, 1987). For many years, it was generally believed that sophisticated readers sampled text. Based on predictions about what words and letters they would see, readers were thought to look at the words and letters just enough to see if their predictions were confirmed. Eye-movement research carried out with computerized tracking has proven that, in reality, readers look at every word and almost every letter of each word. The amount of time spent processing each letter is incredibly small, only a few hundredths of a second. The astonishingly fast letter recognition for letters within familiar words and patterns is explained by the fact that our brains expect certain letters to occur in sequence with other letters.

Readers usually recode printed words into sound (Cunningham and Cunningham, 1978; Tannenhaus, Flanigan, and Seidenberg, 1980; McCutchen, Bell, France, and Perfetti, 1991). Although it is possible to read without any internal speech, we rarely do. Most of the time as we read, we think the words in our mind. This phonological information is then checked with the information we received visually by analyzing the word for familiar spelling patterns. Saying the words aloud or thinking the words also seems to perform an important function in holding the words in auditory memory until enough words are read to create meaning.

Readers recognize most words immediately and automatically without using context (LaBerge amd Samuels, 1974; Perfetti, 1985; Stanovich, 1980, 1986, 1991; Samuels, 1988; Nicholson, 1991). Good readers use context to see if what they are reading makes sense. Context is also important for disambiguating the meaning of some words (I had a *ball* throwing the *ball* at the *ball*.) Occasionally, readers use context to figure out what the word is. Most of the time, however, words are identified based on their familiar spelling and the association of that spelling with a pronunciation. Context comes into play after, not before, the word is identified based on the brain's processing of the letter-by-letter information it receives. Several studies have found that poor readers rely more on context than good readers.

Readers accurately and quickly pronounce infrequent, phonetically regular words (Perfetti and Hogaboam, 1975; Hogaboam and Perfetti, 1978; Daneman, 1991). When presented with unfamiliar but phonetically regular words—*drite, chinique*—good readers immediately and seemingly effortlessly assign them a pronunciation. (*Drite* begins like *draw* and rhymes with *write*. It is a wonderful neologism for what four-year-olds do when they combine drawing and writing. *Chinique* is a much-needed word which combines the qualities of *chic and unique*. A jacket that is chinique is in style and uniquely you!) The ability to quickly and accurately pronounce phonetically, regular words that are not sight words is a task that consistently discriminates among good and poor readers.

Readers use spelling patterns and analogy to decode words (Adams, 1990; Goswami and Bryant, 1990). The answer to the question of whether phonics should be taught in a synthetic or analytic manner seems to be neither. Synthetic approaches generally teach children to go letter-by-letter, assigning a pronunciation to each letter and then blending the individual letters together. Analytic approaches teach rules and are usually filled with confusing jargon. (The *e* on the end makes the vowel long.) Brain research, however, suggests that the brain is a pattern detector, not a rule applier and that, while we look at single letters, we are looking at them considering all the letter patterns we know. Successfully decoding a word occurs when the brain recognizes a familiar spelling pattern or, if the pattern itself is not familiar, searches through its store of words with similar patterns.

To decode the unfamiliar word *knob*, for example, the child who knew many words that began with *kn* would immediately assign to the *kn* the "n" sound. The initial *kn* would be stored in the brain as a spelling pattern. If the child knew only a few other words with *kn* and hadn't read these words very often, that child would probably not have *kn* as a known spelling pattern and thus would have to do a quick search for known words which began with *kn*. If the child found the words *know* and *knew* and then tried this same sound on the unknown word *knob*, that child would have used the analogy strategy. Likewise, the child might know the pronunciation for *ob* because of having correctly read so many words containing the *ob* spelling pattern or might have had to access some words with *ob* to use them to come up with the pronunciation. The child who had no stored spelling patterns for *kn* or *ob* and no known words to access and compare to would be unlikely to successfully pronounce the unknown word *knob*.

Readers divide big words as they see them based on interletter frequencies (Mewhort and Campbell, 1981; Seidenberg, 1987). The research on syllabication rules show that it is quite possible to know the rules and still be unable to quickly and accurately pronounce novel polysyllabic words and equally possible to be able to pronounce them and not know the rules. Good readers do "chunk" or divide words into manageable units. They do this based on the brain's incredible knowledge of which letters usually go together in words. If you did not recognize the word *midnight* in print, you would divide it as you saw it, between the *d* and the *n*. For the word *Madrid*, however, you would divide after the *a*, leaving the *dr* together. Interletter frequency theory explains this neatly by pointing out that the letters *dr* often occur together in syllables in words you know (*drop*, *dry*, *Dracula*). Words with the letters *dn* in the same syllable are almost nonexistent. This also explains why beginners might pronounce f-a-t-h-e-r as "fat her" but children who have some words from which the brain can generate interletter frequencies will leave the *th* together and pronounce "father."

To summarize what the brain does to identify words is to run the risk of oversimplification, but seems necessary before considering what we know about instruction. As we read, we look very quickly at almost all letters of each word. For most words, this visual information is recognized as a familiar pattern with which a spoken word is identified and pronounced. Words we have read before are instantly recognized as we see them. Words we have not read before are almost instantly pronounced based on spelling patterns the brain has seen in other words. If the word is a big word, the brain uses its interletter frequency knowledge (based on all the words it knows) to chunk the word into parts whose letter patterns can then be compared. Meaning is accessed through visual word recognition, but the sound of the word supports the visual information and helps to hold the word in memory.

WHAT WE KNOW ABOUT HOW CHILDREN LEARN TO READ WORDS

At present, we know more about how the word identification process works than we do about how children learn to do it. Here are some research-based findings which should have an impact on instruction.

Children from literate homes have over 1,000 hours of informal reading and writing encounters before coming to school (Adams, 1990). We have always known that children who were read to came to school more ready, willing, and able to learn to read. In the past decade, however, findings from emergent literacy research have made it clear that the reading/writing encounters many children have include more than just a bedtime story. Estimates are that children from literate homes experience almost an hour each day of informal reading and writing encounters—being read to, trying to read a favorite book, watching someone write a thank-you letter, trying to write, manipulating magnetic letters, talking with someone about environmental print such as grocery/restaurant labels, signs, and so forth. From these encounters, the children learn a tremendous amount of critical information. They know what reading and writing are really for and that you use words and letters. They know that you have to write these words and letters in a particular way, from top to bottom and left to right (though they often don't know this jargon). They also learn some words—important words like their name and the name of their pet dog and favorite fast-food restaurant. They learn the names of many of the letters of the alphabet and write these letters, usually in capital form. In addition to learning that words are made up of letters, which you can see, they somehow figure out that words are also made up of sounds, which you can't see.

Phonemic awareness is critical to success in beginning reading (Bryant, Bradley, Maclean, and Crossland, 1989; Perfetti, 1991). One of the understandings that many children gain from early reading and writing encounters is the understanding that words are made up of sounds. These sounds are not separate and distinct. In fact, their existence is quite abstract. Phonemic awareness has many levels, and includes the ability to hear whether or not words rhyme, to know what word you would have if you removed a sound, and to manipulate phonemes to form different words. Phonemic awareness seems to be developed through lots of exposure to nursery rhymes and books which make words sound fun. Many of the "I can read" books (*Green Eggs and Ham*; *Inside, Outside, Upside Down*; *There's a Wocket in my Pocket*; *The Berenstain Bears B Book*, etc.) which come monthly to the homes of many preschoolers are made to order for helping children develop phonemic awareness. While children may be able to learn some letter sounds before they develop phonemic awareness, phonemic awareness must be present before children can manipulate those sounds as they try to read and write words. Kindergarten and first-grade instruction should include lots of rhymes and chants, writing with invented spelling and sound manipulation games which allow children to figure out the critical relationship between words and phonemes.

Children who can decode well learn sight words better (Jorm and Share, 1983; Stanovich and West, 1989; Ehri, 1991). Research indicates that the sight word versus phonics debate lacks reality when you consider how children learn words. When a new word is encountered for the first time, it is usually decoded. In decoding the word, the child forms phonological access routes for that word into memory. These access routes are built using knowledge of grapheme-phoneme correspondences that connect letters in spelling to phonemes in pronunciations of the words. The letters are processed as visual symbols for the phonemes and the sequence of letters is retained in memory as an alphabetic, phonological representation of the word. When the child encounters that word again, the connections between letters and phonemes is strengthened. Eventually, the spelling is represented in memory and the word is instantly recognized—but that instant recognition was based on some prior phonological processing. So words that were originally decoded come to be recognized as wholes and words originally taught as wholes must be studied letter-by-letter in order to be instantly recognized. The phonics versus sight word debate should be laid to rest.

The division of words into onset and rime is a psychological reality (Trieman, 1985). In the 1934 edition of *Reading and Literature in the Elementary School*, Paul McKee discussed activities to help children decode words and indicated that there was mixed opinion as to whether it was best to start with the initial letters and then add the end (*sa-t*) or to keep the final letters together and add the beginning (*s-at*). Expressing some uncertainty, he did take a stand and recommend the latter. Teachers were encouraged to do word activities in which they took a known word and then changed the initial letters—*hand, sand, band, grand, stand*. [McKee also indicated that "ear training" should precede "eye training" (p. 202) and recommended oral jingles and rhymes, opinions confirmed by phonemic awareness research. Amazingly, he recommended that phonics instruction include "other tools such as analogy. . . ." For example, when confronted with the strange word "meat," he may derive its pronunciation by proper associations gathered from the known words, "eat" and "met" (p. 189).]

McKee's intuitive understanding of the reading process in 1934 led him to recommend what researchers confirmed 50 years later. Syllables are the most distinct sound units in English, and children and adults find it much easier to divide syllables into their onsets (all letters before vowel) and rimes (vowel and what follows) than into any other units. Thus *Sam* is more easily divided into *S-am* than into *Sa-m* or *S-a-m*. It is easier and quicker for people to change *Sam* to *ham* and *jam* than it is to change *Sam* to *sat* and *sad*. The psychological reality of onset and rime confirms the age-old practice of teaching word families and spelling patterns.

Lots of successful reading is essential for readers to develop automaticity and rapid decoding (Samuels, 1988; Stanovich and West, 1989; Juel, 1990; Clay, 1991). The major observable variable that separates good readers from poor readers is that good readers read a lot more and, when they are reading, they recognize most of the words instantly and automatically. If you recognize almost all the words, an unfamiliar word gets your immediate attention and you will stop and figure it out. Lots of easy reading in which most words are immediately recognized is essential for both the development of instantly recognized words and the ability and willingness to decode the occasional unfamiliar word. Many factors—including topic familiarity, text and picture support, number of unfamiliar words and teacher support—interact to determine how easy or difficult a particular book is for a particular child.

Children who write become better readers (Stosky, 1983; Tierney and Leys, 1986). On the face of it, this statement seems almost so obvious as to belie mentioning but in classrooms of a decade ago (and even some today), reading and writing were taught as separate entities. Research shows that the two have a reciprocal relationship and that when they are connected instructionally, children's progress in both is advanced. Young children almost always write the words they can read. As they write, they learn the conventions of reading. Children who write and read always read for meaning because they know that meaning is always what you are trying to communicate when you write. Writers make more sensitive readers and readers make more informed writers.

Children become better decoders when encouraged to invent-spell as they write. Children have been inventing spellings for years but, until recently, those inventions have not been valued in most classrooms. There is still controversy about how long to allow children to continue to invent-spell and whether or not children will move through the stages of invented spelling if they are not given any spelling instruction. Encouraging invented spelling, however, does seem to help children develop decoding skills. Clarke (1988) compared the effectiveness of invented spelling versus an emphasis on correct spelling in first-grade classrooms. The children who had invented spellings were superior to the others on measures of word decoding at the end of the year. Furthermore, this invented spelling/decoding connection was particularly striking for the children who had been designated as having low readiness at the beginning of the year.

My own observations of young children trying to figure out how to spell a word they want to write is that they do indeed say the word slowly and try to listen for the sounds they hear. Listening for the sounds in a word you can say and want to write appears to be easier than using sounds to figure out a word during reading. Thus, children who are encouraged to invent-spell as they write may have a more natural medium for applying whatever letter-sound knowledge they are learning.

What Kind of Phonics Instruction Should We Advocate?

Earlier, I described the coincidence of reading *Beginning to Read* and viewing a Reading Recovery lesson in the same day. As I watched the Reading Recovery lesson, I saw instruction which embodied the theoretical understandings I was gaining from the research. Since then, I have watched many Reading Recovery lessons and studied Clay's (1991, 1994) works and thought about the research/instruction compatibility. I would like to describe for you a beginning Reading Recovery lesson and point out why I think this instruction demonstrates the kind of balance and variety we need.

> **Vincent enters and goes immediately to the chalkboard where he writes from memory several high-frequency words (*to*, *my*, *me*) his teacher dictates. He then selects, from books already read, three books he would like to reread and rereads them with high accuracy and fluency. Next, he rereads the book introduced yesterday while the teacher takes a running record, looking for at least 90 percent accuracy.**

Next, his teacher directs him to make words using magnetic letters. He changes letters around several times to make the rhyming words *me*, *we*, and *he*. He then picks up his writing notebook and rereads two previously written one-sentence stories and matches their cut-up words. He writes a new story based on a book read today. His story is: *The bear squashed the bike.* He writes the words he knows how to spell. For others, the teacher helps him to say the word slowly and write in the letters he can hear and she completes the word with other needed letters. Then, he reads his sentence to the teacher and watches as she writes it on a sentence strip and cuts it into words. He matches these cut-up words to his sentence twice and then uses the cut-up words to make the sentence without matching twice.

The last activity in this packed 30 minutes is the introduction of a new book. The teacher reads and talks through a new predictable book with him. He then reads the new book with teacher assistance.

Each day, Vincent leaves the lesson with an old book to take home. He also takes the cut-up words for his sentence.

Vincent returns to his classroom. His classmates look up expectantly. "What you got today?" some ask. Proudly, Vincent takes out his book which he and his friends read together, with Vincent in the lead. Then, he puts his sentence together and reads. "The bear squashed the bike." The teacher walks over to see "what he's got!" Vincent reads his sentence to the teacher. She comments on how well he is reading and writing and Vincent proudly puts everything back into the zip-lock bag to take home and read some more!

This description of a Reading Recovery lesson doesn't begin to do justice to the intricacies and complexities of the instructional decisions his teacher makes and how she moves him forward each day as he develops his "self-improving system." But, hopefully, it does demonstrate the compatibility of Reading Recovery lessons with research about how word identification abilities develop. Vincent spends most of his time reading and writing. He reads books which are easy, because he has read them many times before, because the teacher is skillful in choosing and introducing them, and because the books are carefully leveled to ensure a high degree of fluency. His writing is supported. He writes the words he can spell automatically and he is supported as he listens for sounds in words he wants to write. The teacher filling in letters he can't know yet means that his sentence is written correctly and he has correct visual representations of the words to put in memory. Working with these words by matching and then using the cut-up words to make his sentence provided the practice needed for these words to become part of his automatic recognition vocabulary. Practice with high-frequency words he has read and written is also provided as he writes a few words on the chalkboard each day. The magnetic letters are used to help him learn some spelling patterns and, more importantly, to learn that there are patterns to be found if you look! Vincent has many opportunities to learn how reading and writing work and all these opportunities are connected to each other and stem from a book he can read. The practice and overlearning provided by reading the book and sentence with his classmates, teacher, and presumably someone at home are also critical for developing fluency and automaticity.

For the past several years, I have worked with first- and second- grade teachers to try to take what we know about how children develop quick, accurate word identification systems and become readers and writers and what we know from the success of Reading Recovery and to develop a classroom model. This model is a multilevel, multimethod approach because we provide numerous methods for children of all different ability levels to learn to read and write (Cunningham, Hall, and Defee, 1991; Cunningham, 1991; Cunningham and Allington, 1994). A key feature of this program is the lack of any fixed ability groups and the division of the 120 to 150 minutes of instructional time into four fairly equal blocks of instruction. We consider each block equally important and, whenever possible, make links across the blocks. The four blocks are: Guided Reading Block—which involves teacher-guided reading and discussion of selections from basal readers and tradebooks; Writing Block—which follow a writing process format; Self-Selected Block—in which the children choose what they want to read from a wide range of books and other reading materials; and the Working With Words Block. Multimethod, multilevel literacy instruction is just one example of how our classrooms might develop balanced literacy programs.

The kind of phonics instruction we need and for which we should advocate is not the "old phonics." It is not rules and jargon and worksheets. The kind of phonics instruction we need must reflect our current understanding of how the brain works and how words are processed and learned. Simultaneously, we must ensure that authentic reading and writing form the core of literacy instruction in every classroom. We must reject the either/or, pro/con stances taken in the past and promote balanced literacy instruction. There is hope that this may be happening. Several articles by leaders in the field of reading advocating for balance have recently been published (Pearson, 1993; Spiegel, 1992; Stahl, 1992). At the International Reading Association in May 1993 a Special Interest Group for Balanced Reading Instruction was formed. At its inaugural meeting, the crowd of people wanting to join was so great the meeting flowed into the hall. Perhaps the controversy McKee referred to in 1934 is finally being put to rest!

References

Adams, M. J. (1990). *Beginning to Read: Thinking and Learning About Print.* Cambridge, MA: MIT Press.

Bryant, P. E., Bradley, L., Maclean, M., and Crossland, I. (1989). Nursery rhymes, phonological skills and reading. *Journal of Child Language*, *16*, 407–428.

Clarke, L. K. (1988). Invented versus traditional spelling in first graders' writings: Effects on learning to spell and read. *Research in the Teaching of English*, *22*, 281–309.

Clay, M. M. (1991). *Becoming Literate: The Construction of Inner Control.* Portsmouth, NH: Heinemann.

Clay, M. M. (1994). *Reading Recovery: A Guidebook for Teachers in Training.* Portsmouth, NH: Heinemann.

Cunningham, P. M. (1975–76). Investigating a synthesized theory of mediated word identification. *Reading Research Quarterly*, *11*, 127–143.

Cunningham, P. M. (1979). A compare/contrast theory of mediated word identification. *The Reading Teacher*, *32*, April, 774–778.

Cunningham, P. M. (1980). Applying a compare/contrast process to identifying polysyllabic words. *Journal of Reading Behavior*, *12*, 213–223.

Cunningham. P. M., and Allington, R. l. (1994). *Classrooms That Work: They Can All Read and Write.* NY: HarperCollins.

Cunningham, P. M. (1991). Research Directions: Multimethod, multilevel literacy instruction in first grade. *Language Arts*, *68*, 578–584.

Cunningham, P. M., and Guthrie, F. M. (1982). Teaching decoding skills to educable mentally handicapped children. *The Reading Teacher*, *35*, February, 1982, 554–559.

Cunningham, P. M., and Cunningham, J. W. (1978). "Investigating the 'Print to Meaning' Hypothesis." In P. D. Pearson and J. Hansen (eds.), *Reading: Disciplined Inquiry in Process and Practice* (Twenty-seventh Yearbook of the National Reading Conference, pp. 116–120). Clemson, SC: National Reading Conference.

Cunningham, P. M., Hall, D. P., and Defee, M. (1991). "Non-ability Grouped, Multilevel Instruction: A Year in a First-grade Classroom." *The Reading Teacher*, *44*, 566–571.

Daneman, M. (1991). "Individual Differences in Reading Skills." In R. Barr, M. L. Kamil, P. B. Mosenthal, and P. D. Pearson, *Handbook of Reading Research* (Vol. 2, pp. 512–538). White Plains, NY: Longman.

Ehri, L. C. (1991). "Development of the Ability to Read Words." In R. Barr, M. L. Kamil, P. B. Mosenthal, and P. D. Pearson, *Handbook of Reading Research* (Vol. 2, pp. 383–417). White Plains, NY: Longman.

Gaskins I. W, Downer, M. A., Anderson, R. C., Cunningham, P. M., Gaskins, R. W., Schommer, M., and the Teachers of the Benchmark School. (1988). "A Metacognitive Approach to Phonics: Using What You Know to Decode What You Don't Know." *Remedial and Special Education*, *9*, 36–41.

Goswami, U., and Bryant, P. (1990). *Phonological Skills and Learning to Read.* East Sussex, UK: Erlbaum Associates.

Hogaboam, T., and Perfetti, C. A. (1978). "Reading Skill and the Role of Verbal Experience in Decoding." *Journal of Verbal Learning and Verbal Behavior*, *70*, 717–729.

Jorm, A. F., and Share, D. L. (1983). "Phonological Recoding and Reading Acquisition." *Applied Psycholinguistics, 4,* 103–147.

Juel, C. (1990). "Effects of Reading Group Assignment on Reading Development in First and Second Grade. *Journal of Reading Behavior, 22,* 233–254.

LaBerge, D., and Samuels, S. J. (1974). "Toward a Theory of Automatic Information Processing in Reading." *Cognitive Psychology, 6,* 293–323.

McKee, P. (1934). *Reading and Literature in the Elementary School.* Boston: Houghton Mifflin.

McClelland, J. L., and Rumelhart, D. E. (eds.) (1986). *Parallel Distributed Processing, Vol. 2: Psychological and Biological Models.* Cambridge, MA: MIT Press.

McConkie, G. W., Kerr, P. W., Reddix, M. D., and Zola, D. (1987). *Eye Movement Control During Reading: The Location of Initial Eye Fixations on Words.* Technical Report No. 406. Champaign, IL: Center for the Study of Reading, University of Illinois.

McCutchen, D., Bell, L. C., France, I. M., and Perfetti, C. A. (1991). "Phoneme-Specific Interference in Reading: The Tongue-Twister Effect Revisited." *Reading Research Quarterly, 26,* 87–103.

Mewhort, D. J. K., and Campbell, A. J. (1981). "Toward a Model of Skilled Reading: An Analysis of Performance in Tachistoscoptic Tasks." In G. E. MacKinnon and T. G. Walker (eds.), *Reading Research: Advances in Theory and Practice, Vol. 3,* 39–118. NY: Academic Press.

Nicholson, T. (1991). "Do children read words better in context or in lists? A classic study revisited." *Journal of Educational Psychology, 83,* 444–450.

Pearson, P. D. (1993). "Teaching and Learning Reading: A Research Perspective." *Language Arts, 70,* 502–511.

Perfetti, C. A. (1985). *Reading Ability.* New York: Oxford University Press.

Perfetti, C. A. (1991). "The Psychology, Pedagogy, and Politics of Reading." *Psychological Science, 2,* 70, 71–76.

Perfetti, C. A., and Hogaboam, T. (1975). "The Relationship Between Single-Word Decoding and Reading Comprehension Skill." *Journal of Educational Psychology, 67,* 461–469.

Rayner, K., and Pollatsek, A. (1989). *The Psychology of Reading.* Englewood Cliffs, NJ: Prentice Hall.

Rumelhart, D. E., and McClelland, J. L. (eds.) (1986). *Parallel Distributed Processing, Vol. 1: Psychological and Biological Models.* Cambridge, MA: MIT Press.

Samuels, S. J. (1988). "Decoding and Automaticity: Helping Poor Readers Become Automatic at Word Recognition." *The Reading Teacher, 41,* 756–760.

Seidenberg, M. S. (1987). "Sublexical Structures in Visual Word Recognition: Access Units or Orthographic Redundancy." In M. Coltheart (ed.), *Attention and Performance XII: The Psychology of Reading,* 245–263, Hillsdale, NJ: Erlbaum Associates.

Seidenberg, M. S., and McClelland, J. L. (1989). "A Distributed, Developmental Model of Word Recognition and Naming." *Psychological Review, 96,* 523–568.

Spiegel, D. L. (1992). "Blending Whole Language and Systematic Direct Instruction." *The Reading Teacher, 46,* 38–48.

Stahl, S. A. (1992). "Saying the 'P' Word: Nine Guidelines for Exemplary Phonics Instruction." *The Reading Teacher, 45,* 618–625.

Stanovich, K. E. (1980). "Toward an Interactive Compensatory Model of Individual Differences in the Development of Reading Fluency." *Reading Research Quarterly*, *16*, 32–71.

Stanovich, K. E. (1986). "Matthew Effects in Reading: Some Consequences of Individual Differences in the Acquisition of Literacy." *Reading Research Quarterly*, *21*, 360–406.

Stanovich, K. E. (1991). "Word Recognition: Changing Perspectives." In R. Barr, M. L. Kamil, P. B. Mosenthal, and P. D. Pearson, *Handbook of Reading Research* (Vol. 2, pp. 418–452). White Plains, NY: Longman.

Stanovich, K. E., and West, R. F. (1989). "Exposure to Print and Orthographic Processing." *Reading Research Quarterly*, *24*, 402–433.

Stosky, S. (1983). "Research on Reading/Writing Relationships: A Synthesis and Suggested Directions." *Language Arts, 60,* 627–642.

Tannenhaus, M. K., Flanigan, H., and Seidenberg, M. S. (1980). "Orthographic and Phonological Code Activation in Auditory and Visual Word Recognition." *Memory and Cognition, 8,* 513–520.

Tierney, R. J., and Leys, M. (1986). "What Is the Value of Connecting Reading and Writing?" In B. T. Peterson (ed.) *Convergences: Transactions in Reading and Writing* (pp. 15–29). Urbana, IL: National Council of Teachers of English.

Trieman, R. (1985). "Onsets and Rimes as Units of Spoken Syllables: Evidence from Children. *Journal of Experimental Child Psychology, 39,* 161–181.

INDEX